Polyamory and Reading
the Book of Ruth

Feminist Studies and Sacred Texts Series

Series Editor: Susanne Scholz (sscholz@mail.smu.edu)

Advisory Board: Naomi Appleton, Tamara Cohn Eskenazi, Lynn Huber, Sa'diyya Shaikh, and Sharada Sugirtharajah

Feminist Studies and Sacred Texts makes available innovative and provocative research on the interface of feminist studies and sacred texts. Books in the series are grounded in religious studies perspectives, theories, and methodologies, while engaging with the wide spectrum of feminist studies, including women's studies, gender studies, sexuality studies, masculinity studies, and queer studies. They embrace intersectional discourses such as postcolonialism, ecology, disability, class, race, and ethnicity studies. Furthermore, they are inclusive of religious texts from both established and new religious traditions and movements, and they experiment with inter- and cross-religious perspectives. The series publishes monographs and edited collections that critically locate feminist studies and sacred texts within the historical, cultural, sociological, anthropological, comparative, political, and religious contexts in which they were produced, read, and continue to shape present practices and discourses.

Titles in Series

Polyamory and Reading the Book of Ruth

Deborah Kahn-Harris

LEXINGTON BOOKS
Lanham • Boulder • New York • London

Published by Lexington Books
An imprint of The Rowman & Littlefield Publishing Group, Inc.
4501 Forbes Boulevard, Suite 200, Lanham, Maryland 20706
www.rowman.com

86-90 Paul Street, London EC2A 4NE

British Library Cataloguing in Publication Information Available

Library of Congress Cataloging-in-Publication Data

Names: Kahn-Harris, Deborah, author.
Title: Polyamory and reading the Book of Ruth / Deborah Kahn-Harris.
Description: Lanham, Maryland : Lexington Books, [2024] | Series: Feminist studies and sacred texts series | Includes bibliographical references and index. | Summary: "This book establishes a polyamorous hermeneutic for reading biblical texts and applies it to the Book of Ruth. The book concludes with a contemporary 'targumic' rendition of the Book of Ruth, which foregrounds this polyamorous reading"— Provided by publisher.
Identifiers: LCCN 2023035546 (print) | LCCN 2023035547 (ebook) | ISBN 9781666932096 (cloth) | ISBN 9781666932102 (epub)
Subjects: LCSH: Bible. Ruth—Criticism, interpretation, etc. | Non-monogamous relationships.
Classification: LCC BS1315.52 .K34 2024 (print) | LCC BS1315.52 (ebook) | DDC 222/.3506—dc23/eng/20230818
LC record available at https://lccn.loc.gov/2023035546
LC ebook record available at https://lccn.loc.gov/2023035547

Contents

Preface

This book began with a straightforward realization—namely, that as a cis-gender woman in a heteronormative monogamous marriage, I have been socialized to read all romantic stories as though they were my story. Unconsciously, I have always assumed that when reading a potential love story, the aim of the narrative is, eventually, for it to resolve into the "happily ever after" ending: a dyadic coupling resulting in socially sanctioned (religious or secular) marriage and children. I know that sometimes these stories deliberately play on the genre and, hence, end differently—the "twist" is that the "happily ever after" coupling is actually a same-sex couple or that a cisgender woman could end up on her own, "happily ever after" without the man, and so on—but what I had never truly considered was that the "happily ever after" might actually involve something other than a dyadic coupling. I never considered this possibility because it's just not the way mainstream romance stories have been told in the English-speaking world for the last two hundred years or so, since the romance novel (and its subsequent iterations like the rom-com film) became part of the mainstream culture. Love stories are always about couples, whether they are getting their relationship right or not.

So I never thought, "Huh, what happens if instead of choosing between her two suitors, she chooses them both and they end up, all three of them, happily ever after," or "Maybe instead of settling down into two couples, who have to give up something of themselves in order to be in that couple, they would just be a lot happier as a foursome sharing out the emotional load," or various other options. But the world is changing, and with it, my notions of what a happy ending might look like.

Multiple-person households are no strangers to the Hebrew Bible. Polygamy, as I will discuss, is a standard feature of the biblical narrative. Polygamy, however, is not polyamory, and while the term *polyamory* is of recent construction, the idea that it presents is surely not new at all—that more than two people can form a loving, emotionally supportive relationship that sustains them (and any progeny they may have) over a substantial period of time. The question then arises within the biblical context: How might someone have coded a story of a "happily ever after" for a relationship involving more than two people? In a text so heavily invested in patriarchy and all that flows from it, how would a story of genuine love and care in a multiperson household actually be told? And how would those of us so heavily conditioned to read for dyadic, socially and religiously sanctioned marriage, be able to listen to the hints that a different story was being told? What would happen if I listened to a different story than the one I had always *assumed* I was reading? Would I hear a hidden transcript breaking out of the text?

None of which is meant to assert that my reading of the Book of Ruth is any truer than any of the readings that have come before, but I would argue vociferously that my reading is no less true either. I have also been socialized to read in a midrashic fashion, in which every reading, every interpretation, is only a *davar acher* (another matter), whose truth value is no less great than the interpretation that immediately precedes it. So I consider my interpretation of the Book of Ruth just that, a *davar acher*, a concept alongside other rabbinic modes of reading, which I will unpack in greater detail in due course.

In the end, this book is based on a simple premise: What if the Book of Ruth isn't a love story in the vein of Jane Austen, Thomas Hardy, or even a Jennifer Aniston rom-com? What if the Book of Ruth is still a love story, just not the way so many of us have been taught to read it?

Finally, all translations in this book are my own, unless otherwise noted (most of which are from the New Jewish Publication Society translation [NJPS]).

Acknowledgments

I want to thank my family for putting up with me as I worked on this book. According to my (then) teenage children, the only thing more embarrassing than having a father who writes books about the warning messages in Kinder Surprise Eggs is having a mother who writes about "throuples in the Bible" (absolutely not my language). I accept that at the age when most people are still working out their sexuality (in private and certainly not discussing it with their parents), having a mother who openly discusses the various ways in which people might form lasting relationships is probably the height of social awkwardness. I hope that, in the fullness of time, they will be proud of my work nevertheless. And to my husband, Keith, I simply could not have done this without your unwavering support and belief in me. Here is hoping we both write many more books.

I would also like to express my most profound thanks to Dr. Stephen Herman z'l and the Board of Governors of Leo Baeck College for finally, after more than ten years in post, granting me a sabbatical during which time I was able to complete the first draft of this book. Additionally, I would not have been able to take sabbatical time without the support of the whole staff and the faculty of Leo Baeck College, who ensured that the day-to-day running of the college continued seamlessly and expertly in my absence. In particular, the senior management team—Rabbi Dr. Charles Middleburgh, Dr. Jo-Ann Myers, Gaby Ruppin, and Bill Varon—were and continue to be the best of colleagues.

My thanks to my editors at Lexington Books—Trevor F. Crowell, who originally suggested to me that I develop my SBL 2021 paper into this book, and Megan White, who inherited my proposal following Trevor's departure. My thanks to both for sticking with me.

I must also extend my profoundest gratitude to Professor Johanna Stiebert and Rabbi Nikki DeBlosi, who helped to calm my nerves and gave freely and generously of their time to ensure that this book is far better than it might otherwise have been. They both exemplify what it means to be a critical friend and colleague. Finally, I want to express not merely my thanks but also my heartfelt awe for her talent to Tilla Crowne (https://tilla.co.uk/), whose exceptional artwork graces the cover of this book. The artwork that has grown out of our conversations is more than I could ever have hoped for and presents its own, very beautiful interpretation of the Book of Ruth.

Introduction

Why write another book about the Book of Ruth? So much ink has already been spilled commenting on it that the commentaries have long since far outweighed the mere four chapters of the book itself. Can there be anything left to say at all?

For me, one of the gifts of the Hebrew Bible, and particularly short works such as the Book of Ruth, is the terseness of the text that creates lacunae to interpret, the sorts of in-between spaces from which meaning can erupt. In the rabbinic tradition, this abundance of meaning is drawn from Jer. 23:29: "Behold, My word is like fire—declares the Eternal One—and like a hammer that shatters rock!" In *B. Sanhedrin* 34a, the school of Rabbi Yishmael teaches that "like a hammer that breaks the rock in pieces, just as [the rock] is split into many splinters, so also may one biblical verse convey many teachings." So, yes, for if even just a single verse may convey many meanings, then how much more so can the Book of Ruth, an entire book of verses, convey a wide multiplicity of meanings?

Over many years of teaching the Book of Ruth, I have read a great many of these possible interpretations. And as I have read, taught, and learned from my students, I have thought more deeply about my own interpretation of this work. The interpretation I offer here is not, in my view, "the most correct" or "best" interpretation—only one in a long line of possible understandings of the book, rooted in my experience of reading and teaching, and one that I hope will resonate with a contemporary generation of readers. I offer it here as a possibility, as another splinter from the rock of the text, another spark off the hammer of interpretation.

READING RUTH FOR RELATIONSHIPS

Reading Ruth for relationships begins with the premise that at the core of the story is a character-driven narrative that navigates the interrelationships among a cast of characters—not only the "main" characters but the widest range of people reflected in the text. Each of these people—named and unnamed, individuals and collectives—has a role to play in determining the various relationships (including and especially the family units) in the text. I want to challenge the ways in which the text has been read previously as coming from particular, socially constructed notions of what constitutes personal and familial relationships that, at least until fairly contemporary times, have privileged heteronormativity. Crucially, I want to examine what happens when interpretation moves beyond the imagination of a resolution to the narrative based solely on the dyadic coupling of cisgender individuals, as many (if not most) of us have been conditioned to read.

In reading Ruth for relationships in this fashion, I will draw on a number of different hermeneutical frameworks, including queer studies and traditional Jewish modes of interpretation. I will explicate subsequently the ways in which I will use each of these methodologies to inform my reading.

But, importantly, I am not reading as a queer person myself.[1] I am a cis woman in a long-standing monogamous marriage with (nearly adult) children, albeit one who considers herself both an ally to the LGBTQIA+ community and a feminist.[2] I hope that I am reading with sensitivity to people and communities that identify with the elements that I detect in the story. As a rabbi (of a liberal—both religious and political—affiliation and mind-set), I hope that reading Ruth for relationships that encompass a wider range of family units and gender identities will enable people who have not heard their stories in the biblical text before to find in the Book of Ruth a new opportunity to find their lives reflected in the text, even in some small way.

That being said, I did not purposefully set out to search for a reading that would be inclusive in this fashion. I came to this reading through deep engagement with the text. In the end, I came to this reading because it makes sense to me, because the more I engage with reading Ruth, the more I have come to believe that reading it as though it were a nineteenth-century romance novel (or something similar) is doing an injustice to the text itself.

READING BEYOND DYADS

According to Esther Saxey,

> The notion of monogamy in literature as the reflection of a natural phenomenon does not stand up for long. Even if we were to assume that monogamy

is an unremarkable, static aspect of culture, it is not a static element in fiction. Monogamy is a dynamic presence in fiction, constructed and contested in individual texts and in generic norms. . . . (Non-)monogamy structures plots; its establishment, failure or restoration, form the climactic scenes of many texts.[3]

For many readers, Saxey's assertion may come as a surprise. The notion that not all romantic relationships in literature will eventually resolve themselves into monogamous, dyadic relationships (and most commonly heterosexual ones) goes against the grain of how most contemporary readers are socialized to read, as well as consume film and television. One needs to think only of the myriad of television dating programs currently available, in which the tension is built entirely around the assumption of monogamous, dyadic coupling.

Yet non-dyadic relationships in the form of polygamy are, perhaps surprisingly, fairly common in the Hebrew Bible.[4] Abraham is married to Sarah but has a child by her maidservant, Hagar, at Sarah's urging.[5] Jacob is married to Leah *and* Rachel, both of whom bring their maidservants, Bilhah and Zilpah, into the relationship.[6] Elkanah is married to both Hannah and Peninnah.[7] Both King David and King Solomon had multiple wives.[8] The Levite at the end of the Book of Judges has a secondary wife, whose story is essential to the end of the book.[9] Indeed, while Biblical Hebrew's term for wife, אִשָּׁה (*'sāh*), is the same word for "woman" more generally, Biblical Hebrew has a separate term for "secondary wife," פִּלֶגֶשׁ (*Plegeōs*), so common was the practice.[10]

Yet referring to such relationships as "non-dyadic" would be misleading. More accurate would be to say that the male character in each of these polygamous relationships has a series of dyadic relationships with each of the women involved. Indeed, far from there being any implication that the multiple wives and secondary wives had some sort of emotionally supportive bond with each other, many of the stories told overtly suggest open hostility between the women involved in these marriages.[11] Sarah eventually demands that Abraham cast out Hagar and her son by Abraham, Ishmael. Leah and Rachel compete to provide sons for Jacob, providing Bilhah and Zilpah for extra fertility. Rachel, beloved and desired by Jacob, cannot easily become pregnant and bear children. Leah, whom Jacob never intended to marry in the first place, conceives easily. So fierce is their rivalry, competition, and ensuing dislike of each other that it is the assumed reason behind biblical law subsequently forbidding sister marriage.[12] Peninnah is depicted as taunting Hannah, who, like Rachel, is loved by her husband but suffers from infertility.[13] The Levite's secondary wife returns to her father's house because she is so unhappy in her marriage. Despite running after her to retrieve her, the Levite sends her out to the braying mob to be raped to death in order to save his own skin.

None of these stories, nor any of the other similar ones in the Hebrew Bible, inspires much confidence that a marriage with multiple partners can be a happy one. These stories serve to reinforce the sense that the purpose of polygamy is to allow men in a patriarchal society to increase the number of their progeny. Moreover, all of these examples reinforce the idea that polygamous marriages offer little to the women involved and, even worse, serve as a source of hostility for female relationships. And if the women involved have problems with their relationships with each other, those of the next generation likewise find themselves, sometimes with their mothers' aid, battling for inheritance rights and (in the case of David) succession to the throne.[14] Jacob's sons go so far as to sell their father's favorite son, Joseph, by his beloved wife, Rachel, into slavery. Altogether, biblical polygamy as a model for non-dyadic relationships is a poor advert for emotionally well-connected families, let alone a fully engaged relationship between multiple (more than two) adults who can sustain each other in a loving relationship.

Clearly, contemporary forms of polyamory, particularly when consciously constructed as an ethical practice, are something very different from biblical polygamy. Understanding how contemporary polyamorous relationships are constructed can serve as a useful starting point for helping us recognize the clues for how these relationships might look in the biblical text.

Contemporary polyamorous relationships are diverse. They may be open or closed relationships—that is, the multiple partners may have other relationships (sexual and/or emotional, short or long term) with people outside of their polyamorous relationship, or the partners may all agree to sexual and emotional fidelity within the confines of the polyamorous relationship. Members of polyamorous relationships may present with a wide array of gender identities, such as cis, transgender, nonbinary, genderfluid, genderqueer, pangender, and so on.[15] They may identify with any of the myriad possible sexual orientations, such as lesbian, gay, bisexual, straight, pansexual, asexual, demisexual, and so forth. Polyamorous relationships include more than two individuals, but no upper limit exists on how many people may be involved. The construction of the relationship is determined entirely by its members. And just as in dyadic relationships, sexual activity is only one aspect of the relationship. Emotional support, child rearing, housework, financial interdependency, social care, and much more also contribute to the bonds that tie people together.

Although being part of a polyamorous relationship does not require any particular gender identity or sexual orientation from any of the members of the group, contemporary polyamorous practices appear to be more prevalent in LGBTQIA+ communities.[16] Indeed, for genderfluid, genderqueer, and trans people, polyamorous relationships often offer greater opportunities to express their identities and orientations more fully:

> Trans people in polyamorous relationships have wider opportunities to per-
> form gender. That is not to say that trans people are "testing out" gender,
> but rather are able to express a wider variety of gendered presentations
> due the number of intimate relationships available to them. Trans people in
> polyamorous relationships, therefore, have more opportunity for epistemic
> action within these relationships and, potentially, a greater chance to become
> self-actualized.[17]

Indeed, in studies of people in polyamorous relationships, participants have
made statements such as "Each of my lovers interacts with my genderqueer-
ness in a different way, not least because most of them have somewhat fluid
or non-conventional gender presentation as well."[18]

Another part of a polyamorous hermeneutic, therefore, will need to involve
looking consciously for the coding of gender identity within the text. The
Hebrew Bible does not overtly define the gender identity of characters. As
a result, and given the patriarchal framework of the text as well, until very
modern times, most characters have been assumed to be cisgender hetero-
sexuals.[19] Yet not every biblical character easily or comfortably conforms to
such stereotypes.[20]

The attentive reader will notice small details in the characters' descriptions. For example, in Gen. 25:27, Jacob is described as אִישׁ תָּם (*ʾîš tām*), a
simple or decent man, who stays in the camp, in contrast to his brother Esau,
a skilled hunter who enjoys the outdoors. Rabbi Jay Michaelson, attentive to
this single verse detailing the differences between the twins, described Jacob
at this point in his life as "gender non-conforming."[21] Esau is the manly man,
hunting and providing food for his family; Jacob is an effete homebody. In
the Book of Esther, Mordecai is another example, less so because of what
the text says about him than because of what it does *not* say. Mordecai is
described only by his genealogy, with no physical description or comment on
his personality. More curious still are the lacunae in his biography; Mordecai
appears to be unmarried and to have no children of his own until he adopts
the orphaned Hadassah/Esther. Why isn't Mordecai married with his own
children? What should a reader draw from this absence in the text?[22]

David, too, is another especially intriguing example, given that he is
engaged in a polygamous marriage with multiple wives (as noted previously)
and has a relationship with Jonathan that appears to go beyond the bounds
of mere friendship.[23] On learning of the death of Saul and Jonathan, David
laments his loss with a dirge: "I grieve for you,/My brother Jonathan,/You
were most dear to me./Your love was wonderful to me/More than the love
of women" (2 Sam. 1:26).[24] According to Rabbi Steve Greenberg, the first
openly gay Orthodox rabbi, "While the story [of David and Jonathan] drips
with obvious homoeroticism, there is no evidence of any physical intimacy

between them. There is, however, also no evidence in the language that would absolutely preclude such a relationship either."[25]

So here are three examples of men whose gender coding is not as "straight"forward as that of "cisgender, heterosexual men." Mordecai, at least within the confines of the biblical text, never marries. But both Jacob and David end up in polygamous marriages to multiple women. Could we read Mordecai as asexual? Could we read Jacob as gender nonconforming? Might we read David as bisexual (or at least bi-curious)? Might we consider how these possible identities and orientations could have affected David's and Jacob's polygamous marriages?[26] Although that is not the focus of this study, asking questions about David's pursuit of Bathsheba in light of his sexual orientation, or the unhappy state of Jacob's marriage to Rachel and Leah in light of his own gender identity, could be fascinating. Clearly, the sexual orientations and gender identities of these men might well have influenced their polygamous marriages.

So how does polygamous marriage function within the Hebrew Bible, and could it really be viewed as a form of polyamory? Patheos.com blogger Chris McKnight (who blogs as the "Hippie Heretic") differentiates clearly between patriarchal polygamy and polyamorous polygamy within the biblical framework.[27] He outlines five key differences between the two:

1. *Polyamorous* polygamy is based on the love one person has for multiple partners. However, *patriarchal* polygamy is often based on pragmatism or cultural expectations: one or more of the multiple wives may be merely a means to an end, such as to produce a male heir, to establish one's social standing, or to maintain ties with another nation or family.
2. *Polyamorous* polygamy is based on the equality of all people. However, *patriarchal* polygamy is based on the hierarchical ranking of men over women.
3. *Polyamorous* polygamy treats all partners as their own distinct persons. However, *patriarchal* polygamy often treats wives as little more than property.
4. *Polyamorous* polygamy can be polygynous or polyandrous (or it can, for that matter, be same-sex or bisexually oriented). However, *patriarchal* polygamy will almost always be polygynous.
5. *Polyamorous* polygamy is entered into with the full knowledge and free consent of every partner involved. However, *patriarchal* polygamy is entered into primarily at the discretion of the husband; wives may or may not have any say about what additional wives the husband may take.[28]

A key for reading biblical stories of polygamy, therefore, is to differentiate between McKnight's patriarchal and polyamorous forms of polygamy.[29]

I would like to go slightly further in clarifying that within the bounds of this inquiry, I understand that for the purpose of this book, polyamorous polygamy is typified by polyfidelity.[30] *Polyfidelity* describes any polyamorous relationship that is closed to new members (unless consent from all parties involved is obtained) and in which all members are sexually faithful to each other.[31] Polyfidelity, by its very nature, excludes patriarchal polygamy, as in a patriarchal polygamous marriage, the man is free to add as many female partners as he likes without the consent of any of the women involved.[32]

While accepting that overlaying the ways in which any current form of ethical nonmonogamy is practiced onto the biblical text can only be anachronistic, we can nevertheless attempt to ask how, in a patriarchal society that is heavily invested in cisgender, heterosexual cultural norms, a relationship that did not fit this mold might have been encoded in the text.[33] What would a functional polyamorous polygamous relationship look like if we could find it in the Hebrew Bible? How would we know that we had found it?

To the best of my knowledge, the practice of some form of polyamorous hermeneutic has not been consciously described in biblical studies to date. For the purposes of this study, then, I understand a polyamorous hermeneutic to be a reading practice that consciously resists the assumption that all relationships described in the biblical text are fundamentally dyadic and heteronormative.[34] A polyamorous hermeneutic, as an extension of feminist and queer readings of the Bible, enjoins us, as readers, to attune our ears to what might be lying beneath the patriarchal exterior of the text. A polyamorous reading asks us to accept that we are not the first generation of humans to discover the vast panoply of human sexual and emotional desires and to create interpersonal relationships arranged to meet those needs.

Adapting from McKnight's aforementioned distinctions, a polyamorous hermeneutic will ask the following questions:

1. Does each of the individuals in the relationship express regard for each other?
2. What is the power dynamic between each of the individuals in the relationship? Is it exclusively hierarchical, with men having power over the women involved?
3. How do the individuals in the relationship treat one another—as distinct human beings or as chattel?
4. What might the gender identity and sexual orientation of the individuals in the relationship be?
5. Is the relationship consensual for all individuals involved?[35]

In addition to McKnight, I want to borrow from the hermeneutical strategy laid out by Deryn Guest in *When Deborah Met Jael: Lesbian Biblical Hermeneutics*. Guest lists four key hermeneutical strategies:

1. Resistance: commitment to a hermeneutic of hetero-suspicion
2. Rupture: commitment to the disruption of sex-gender binaries
3. Reclamation: commitment to strategies of appropriation
4. Reengagement: commitment to making a difference[36]

Building on Schüssler Fiorenza's well-established feminist hermeneutic of suspicion, Guest creates a "specifically refined version . . . [which] draws critically upon the insights and principles that have already been established while appreciating the contribution that new lesbian critical studies can offer."[37] Guest seeks to expose "the way in which the hetero-patriarchal bias of both text and the history of interpretation has operated."[38] In particular,

> [c]ommitment to a hermeneutic of hetero-suspicion means that the researcher is resistant to the presentation of any storyworld where female homoerotic relations are virtually absent and seeks to problematize that apparent absence. And in those few cases where the possibility of female homoeroticism *is* raised, a hermeneutic of hetero-suspicion is resistant to the portrayal of such relationships as unnatural, sinful or "other."[39]

Beyond being attentive to the issues raised in the hermeneutic of hetero-suspicion, a polyamorous hermeneutic seeks to resist any narrative in which polyamory is absent and seeks to challenge the assumption of dyadic monogamy as the only possible resolution to any romantic relationship plotline. Where any cases that could be read as polyamorous do exist, the polyamorous hermeneutic resists the reading of polyamorous relationships as "unnatural, sinful or 'other.'"

Writing in 2005, Guest's configuration of the disruption of sex-gender binaries prefigures many of the most current conversations around sex and gender. Guest is particularly concerned with the tension between advocating for "the rupture of sex-gender binaries while holding to a specifically *lesbian*-identified interpretative position."[40] As Guest goes on to explain, she is not embracing "strategic essentialism," but rather invoking Judith Butler to destabilize the meaning of what the term "lesbian" actually signifies.[41] In this fashion, "lesbian" becomes "a site for resistant agency."[42] Moreover, she states that

> [e]mbracing a lesbian identity can thus lend support to the idea that hetero and homosexual are stable identities to which one is oriented. . . . A lesbian-identified hermeneutic must . . . be alert for ways of rupturing the homo-hetero binary and to the dangers of using hermeneutical strategies that perpetuate and cement rigid sex, gender and sexuality boundaries.[43]

Although Guest does not explicitly mention the panoply of gender identities that might rupture these boundaries, they are clearly implied here.

Polyamorous relationships, particularly between individuals of differing gender identities, inherently destabilize gender binaries.[44] A polyamorous hermeneutic consciously resists defining individuals as either homo or hetero, cis- or transgender, in favor of more nuanced readings of both sexual orientation and gender identity. Additionally, a polyamorous hermeneutic requires asking multiple questions (e.g., not only to whom are people sexually attracted but also with whom do people create bonds of emotional attachment?). A polyamorous hermeneutic seeks to ascertain how sexual desire and attraction and emotional connection and dependence intersect to create lasting familial relations.

As for the work of reclamation, feminist, queer, postcolonial, minority, and many other readers have been critiquing the work of the supposed "neutral" historical-critical school of biblical hermeneutics for some time. Owing to the predominance of largely cisgender, straight, white European (or European-descended), and most often Christian males over biblical scholarship for generations, assumptions about the sexual orientation and gender identity of biblical characters have overwhelmingly favored the view that characters reflect the identity of these commentators, but, as Guest challenges, "as if historical-critical exegesis were miraculously impartial and non-committal, producing universally applicable interpretations of texts."[45] Still left off this list of norms is "dyadically coupled." Just as queer commentators have had to challenge the assumption of heterosexuality, so, too, a polyamorous hermeneutic resists the assumption of dyadic relationships and disrupts the attendant presumptions about the ways in which human beings form attachments to each other. Particularly within the biblical world in which polygamous marriage is both legal and commonplace, a polyamorous hermeneutic seeks to reclaim the possibilities inherent within a multiple-person "marital" household.

Finally, asking how a polyamorous hermeneutic can "reengage" and "make a difference" is essential. Guest writes that her view is

> that a lesbian-identified hermeneutic that is committed to making a difference, grounded in local contexts and theorized within the academy, would find a welcoming and thriving home in the *métissage*—an umbrella space for those committed to social, political, economic and religious justice and transformation.[46]

Assuming, as I do, that Guest is correct, I believe that a polyamorous hermeneutic has the potential to make a profound difference—not merely toward furthering the acceptance of polyamorous people and families within our communities but also, and perhaps more important, toward ensuring that more people can see their lives reflected in our sacred scriptures. As both a Bible scholar and Principal of Leo Baeck College, a rabbinic training seminary in the United Kingdom, my own career spans both the academy and community life. While I may not personally identify as polyamorous, I live and work in communities that include polyamorous families.[47] Reading the Book of Ruth through a polyamorous hermeneutic is part of my own commitment to and solidarity with those families who have too often had to live at the margins, trying to fit their lives into religious and secular worlds that are oriented toward monogamous, dyadic marriage.[48]

The origins of this book began with the teaching that I conducted both in my seminary and in informal education classes across my community. I then formulated my thinking into a paper, which I delivered first at the Society for Old Testament Study at the summer 2021 conference and then refined for delivery at the Society for Biblical Literature's Annual Meeting in November 2021. On every occasion when I have taught this material, the experience has been overwhelmingly positive, both from people who personally recognize themselves in this interpretation of the story and from people who simply desire their communities to be more inclusive and their sacred text to have the potential to be more reflective of the communities in which they live.[49]

A polyamorous hermeneutic is, therefore, more than just a hermeneutical tool. It is an act of solidarity and a means of (further) opening up boundaries and norms within faith communities for whom the Hebrew Bible remains a core text.[50]

READING LIKE A RABBI

In Barry Holtz's classic work on Jewish texts, he explains:

> The rabbis throughout Jewish history were essentially *readers*. The text was the Torah; the task to read that text. We tend to think of reading as a passive occupation, but for the Jewish textual tradition, it was anything but that. Reading was a passionate and active grappling with God's living word. It held the challenge of uncovering secret meanings, unheard-of explanations, matters of great weight and significance. An active, indeed interactive, reading was their method. . . .
>
> By "interactive" I mean to suggest that for the rabbis of the tradition, Torah called for a living and dynamic response. . . . The Torah remains unendingly alive because the readers of each subsequent generation saw it as such, taking the holiness of the Torah seriously, and adding their own contribution to the story. For the tradition, Torah *demands* interpretation.[51]

This traditional understanding of the role of rabbis and their approach to reading the text of the Hebrew Bible fundamentally underpins my own approach to biblical scholarship. In addition to being trained in the academy as a Hebrew Bible scholar, I am an ordained rabbi, schooled in traditional Jewish modes of reading the biblical text. Like the rabbis of generations past, I, too, believe in the interactive mode of rabbinic reading, which takes the text of the Hebrew Bible seriously and demands interpretation. As such, I want to claim a number of methodological approaches rooted in these traditional rabbinic methods of reading to help inform my interpretation of the Book of Ruth.

To begin, I propose to appropriate the notion of דָּבָר אַחֵר (*davar acher*).[52] The two words mean simply "another matter; another reason; something else."[53] In midrashic literature, *davar acher*, in practice, signifies the completion of one commentary and the beginning of another on the same subject. What is essential about the *davar acher* in midrashic literature in particular is that this second (or third, or fourth, etc.) interpretation is no more or less authoritative than the one(s) that preceded it, even where these interpretations fundamentally conflict with one another. The midrashic imagination allows for multiple conflicting interpretations to coexist without any of them destabilizing the others, a concept known as midrashic polysemy.

Midrashic polysemy is rooted in the commentary found in *B. Sanhedrin* 34a:

> Abaye answered . . . One biblical verse may convey several teachings, but a single teaching cannot be deduced from different biblical verses. In the school of R. Ishmael it was taught: And like in hammer that breaks the rock in pieces [Jer 23:29]: i.e., just as [the rock] is split into many splinters, so also may one biblical verse convey many teachings.

Here the rabbis express their fundamental belief that any single verse (and sometimes even less than a verse) can produce any number of meanings.[54] Although this commentary comes in a longer discussion regarding the production of *halachic* (Jewish legal) rulings, the production of legal norms is more stringently guarded than *aggadic* (non-legal) interpretations of the biblical text. So, if one verse can produce more than one legal norm, it can certainly produce an even wider array of non-legal interpretations. Where these interpretations are entirely unrelated to one another, the phrase *davar acher* is often written at the beginning of a new interpretation to signify that the exegetical process is starting over again with a new idea.

A fairly straightforward example of the use of *davar acher* in practice can be found in *B. Megillah* 14a, which forms part of a midrashic commentary on the Book of Esther. In this passage, we find the recounting of a midrash, which lists the seven prophetesses of the Hebrew Bible.[55] The first of the prophetesses listed is the matriarch, Sarah. The proof text for including her on this list is Gen. 11:29:

וַיִּקַּח אַבְרָם וְנָחוֹר לָהֶם נָשִׁים שֵׁם אֵשֶׁת־אַבְרָם שָׂרָי וְשֵׁם אֵשֶׁת־נָחוֹר מִלְכָּה בַּת־הָרָן אֲבִי־מִלְכָּה וַאֲבִי יִסְכָּה:

Abram and Nahor took for themselves wives, the name of Abram's wife, Sarai, and the name of Nahor's wife, Milcah, the daughter of Haran, the father of Milcah and the father of Iscah.

Why this verse should be the proof text that Sarah is a prophetess is not entirely clear; hence, the following explanation:

וְאָמַר רַבִּי יִצְחָק: "יִסְכָּה" זוֹ שָׂרָה, וְלָמָּה נִקְרָא שְׁמָהּ יִסְכָּה שֶׁסָּכְתָה בְּרוּחַ הַקֹּדֶשׁ, שֶׁנֶּאֱמַר: "כֹּל אֲשֶׁר תֹּאמַר אֵלֶיךָ שָׂרָה שְׁמַע בְּקוֹלָהּ". דָּבָר אַחֵר: "יִסְכָּה" שֶׁהַכֹּל סוֹכִין בְּיוֹפְיָהּ.

And Rabbi Yitzhak said: "Iscah," this is Sarah, and why is she called Iscah because she foresaw through the Holy Spirit, as it is written: "Everything that Sarah will say to you listen to her voice" (Gen. 21:12). Another matter (*davar acher*): "Iscah" because everyone gazed at her beauty.

Briefly, in order to make sense of the use of this verse as a proof text for including Sarah as a prophetess, Rabbi Yitzhak first explains that Sarah is the same person as Iscah. He then goes on to play on the meaning of the root of Iscah (ס.כ.ה.) to explain in what way Sarah behaves as a prophetess. The etymology of Iscah in Biblical Hebrew is uncertain, but Rabbi Yitzhak relies on the meaning of the root in Rabbinic Hebrew, meaning "to look, see, foresee."[56] The first explanation Rabbi Yitzhak gives is that Iscah refers to Gen. 21:12, where God tells Abraham to listen to Sarah's voice, even though she is telling Abraham to cast out Hagar and Ishmael. Sarah is being prescient prophetic in her understanding of what will come, according to this interpretation. Ethically questionable though Sarah's instruction to Abraham is, at least it makes sense as a proof text for her as a prophetess; she is capable of foreseeing the future.

The commentary might have stopped there; instead, we find a *davar acher*, a completely unrelated point. Here, the explanation is not put into the mouth of any particular rabbi. The play on the meaning of the root is still core, but the interpretation is entirely different. Iscah now means that people looked at Sarah because she was beautiful. These two interpretations of the same verse have nothing whatsoever to do with each other. This second interpretation is an entirely different matter, fully a *davar acher*.

What can be demonstrated clearly from this example is that the *davar acher* separates unrelated ideas, allowing space for different textual interpretations to be preserved without impacting each other. In this example, nothing prevents *both* interpretations from being equally and mutually true: Sarah could have both foretold the future *and* also been beautiful. Sometimes, however, the explanations are not mutually compatible but simply preserve different interpretations of one verse.

But there is one other use of the *davar acher* that influences my appropriation of the phrase. In Tannaitic literature, the *davar acher* serves an additional purpose.[57] Occasionally the term is employed as "a euphemism for things which the Talmud does not wish to mention explicitly, either for reasons of modesty or because they were considered repulsive. Accordingly *davar acher* can refer to such things as sexual relations, money, pigs and leprosy."[58]

I am, therefore, claiming that this book is, in its entirety, a *davar acher*. I do not seek to supplant any other interpretation of the Book of Ruth but rather to suggest another matter, another way of looking at the text. My intention is to do so through a sustained, deep engagement with the text that relies not on trying to retrieve its "original" meaning but on trying to ascertain what it *could* mean without, I hope, doing any violence to the text itself. If my readers believe that the text is a heterosexual love story between Ruth and Boaz, or a lesbian love story between Naomi and Ruth, or a narrative argument against the prohibition against marrying Moabites, or a legal story about how levirate marriage worked in practice, or a political tool regarding King David's lineage, or any of the other myriad ways that previous scholars and commentators have proposed reading the text, then this reading should simply be considered another option that in no way seeks to challenge or diminish any of those other readings. Interpretations within the classical rabbinic tradition need not all be mutually compatible, only rooted in the text of the Hebrew Bible.[59] I hope that readers will see this reading as a *davar acher*, another option, for them to consider seriously when they study the text.

Equally, I seek to turn the euphemistic usage of *davar acher* on its head. Where the Talmud sometimes employs *davar acher* to discuss oblique sexual practices outside of its own heteropatriarchal norms, I strive to be open and inclusive, not lewd or prurient, but able to discuss a wide range of human sexual orientations and gender identities without resorting to circumlocution. My intention is that this book, as a *davar acher,* opens up new possibilities for reading the Book of Ruth with frankness about human emotional and sexual relationship building.

The second part of my rabbinic mode of reading is the reclamation of the act of translation, as typified by the Targum. The Targumim (plural of Targum) are a collection of ancient translations of the Hebrew Bible into Aramaic. As the lingua franca of many of the areas throughout which Jews were settled in the early centuries of the Common Era, the translation of the Hebrew Bible into the Aramaic vernacular was important for the transmission of the text. In the ancient synagogue, a *meturgeman* (interpreter) would provide a line-by-line translation of the biblical text when it was read aloud. Eventually, these oral traditions were compiled into official, standardized

Aramaic texts.[60] Although the practice of reading the Targum aloud in synagogues ceased many centuries ago, the practice of reading translations aloud and/or providing a translation of the Hebrew text persists, particularly in English-speaking communities (and especially progressive communities), where knowledge of Biblical Hebrew is often limited.[61]

But whereas English translations of the Hebrew Bible in current use in most synagogues attempt to maintain some sort of literal fidelity to the text (while nevertheless accepting that all translation is, at some level, a form of interpretation), the Targumim demonstrate a different approach to the act of translation. According to Leonard Greenspoon, in discussing the differences between the Septuagint and targumic approaches to translation,

> For the most part, translators into Aramaic were relatively restrained in parting from whatever underlying Hebrew text they had. When they did depart from it, however, it is the case that they exercised considerably more freedom than most Septuagint translators in introducing extensive blocks of "non-biblical" material in both narrative and legal sections. . . . They also incorporated a broad range of updatings to conform to their perceptions of both communal needs and the Oral Tradition.[62]

Étan Levine states more succinctly: "A most remarkable feature characterizing the Aramaic version of the Bible is that whereas some texts are painstakingly literal, others are highly paraphrastic with wide divergence from Scripture."[63] Fundamentally, the Targumim contain much material that is interpolated, creating a text that is both seamlessly translated and interpreted at the same time.

In my final chapter, I will reclaim this targumic approach as a means of "translating" the Book of Ruth for a contemporary audience. Through the "filling in" of textual lacunae identified in my commentary, I will seek to tell a version of the story that makes more explicit the polyamorous possibilities within the story as I read it. The ways in which a story is retold make the potential within it come alive in a fashion that mere interpretation does not. Unlike *midrash*, the more widely known mode of rabbinic interpretation, which has been adopted by many contemporary feminists, in particular, as a means of creating contemporary commentary on the Hebrew Bible, the targumic mode of translation is less prominent today.[64] In choosing the Targum as my model, I want readers to be able to hear the Book of Ruth as a polyamorous tale without the mediation of detailed textual interpretation, just as it was done (albeit with different concerns in mind) by the targumists in antiquity.

At risk, therefore, of falling foul of the Talmudic dictum ascribed to Rabbi Judah in *B. Kiddushin* 49a ("one who translates a verse literally is lying and one who adds to it, behold this one blasphemes"), I have concluded this book with my own "Targum" to the Book of Ruth.[65] In this modern English "Targum," I have interpolated material of my own devising, offering an explicit and unmediated version of my interpretation of the Book of Ruth.[66]

NOTES

1. In this respect, I am grateful to Chris Greenough for his article "'Queer Eye' in Theology and Biblical Studies: 'Do You Have to be Queer to Do This?'" in which he makes a compelling argument for the case that "that there should be no concern about straight-identifying individuals doing queer studies" (26).

2. Although I was married in a Jewish, religious ceremony (in 2001), my husband and I opted not to hold a traditional Jewish wedding; instead, we used a version of the (then) newly constructed egalitarian ceremony constructed by Rachel Adler in her book, *Engendering Judaism*. We did not have a traditional *ketubah* (a Jewish marriage certificate based in Jewish marriage law that understands women as property to be transferred from the ownership of one man to another) but opted for a *brit ahuvim* (literally a "covenant of lovers," which is, like a *ketubah*, a Jewish legal document, but one that is legally rooted in Jewish business partnership law rather than Jewish marriage law) in the affirmation that we intended, and at which we continue to work, for our marriage to be a partnership of equals. Rachel Adler, *Engendering Judaism* (Philadelphia: Jewish Publication Society, 1998), 169–207 and 214–17.

3. Esther Saxey, "Non-monogamy and Fiction," in *Understanding Non-Monogamies*, edited by Meg Barker and Darren Langdridge (New York: Routledge, 2009), 23.

4. Étan Levine, "Biblical Women's Marital Rights," *Proceedings of the American Academy for Jewish Research* 63 (1997): 87–135. While arguing "that monogamy was the reified ideal" (117), he also argues that polygamy was, nevertheless, both normative and, in some cases, preferable, particularly when the options for a woman may have been either to remain in poverty or to become a co-wife to a wealthier man (121–28).

5. Gen. 16. At this point in the story, Abraham is still named Abram and Sarah, Sarai. I have used their names as they are changed in Gen. 17, as these names are the more commonly known ones.

6. Gen. 30:1–24, in particular, although the full story of Leah and Rachel begins in Gen. 29 and ends with Rachel's death in Gen. 35.

7. 1 Sam. 1:1–6, v. 6, in particular.

8. David is married to Michal (1 Sam. 18:17–30), Abigail (1 Sam. 25:39–42), Ahinoam (1 Sam. 25:4:43), and Bathsheba (2 Sam. 11); additionally, Maacah, Haggith, Abital, and Eglah are listed as mothers of David's sons and wives (2 Sam. 3:2–5). According to 1 Kings 11:3, Solomon had "700 royal wives and 300 secondary wives." Naamah is named as the mother of Rehoboam (1 Kings 14:21 and 2 Chron. 21:13).

9. Judg. 19, with the full fallout from the story continuing into Judg. 20 and 21.

10. I use the translation "secondary wife" here rather than the more common translation "concubine," as the latter term has resonances in English that do not entirely

overlap with the term's meaning in the Hebrew Bible. See also David J. A. Clines, ed., *The Dictionary of Classical Hebrew Vol VI* ס – פ (Sheffield: Sheffield Phoenix Press, 2007), 681–82, and Wil Gafney, "Mother Knows Best: Messianic Surrogacy and Sexploitation in Ruth," in *Mother Good, Mother Jones, Mommie Dearest: Biblical Mothers and Their Children*, edited by Cheryl A. Kirk-Duggan and Tina Pippin (Atlanta: SBL, 2009), 28 note 13.

The practice of polygamy was only banned in Jewish communities by Rabbi Gershom ben Judah in c. 1000 CE and even then only initially in western European communities.

11. Cf. Levine, "Biblical Women's Marital Rights," 123:

> Furthermore, co-wives were necessarily "rivals," and the tensions under which women lived were reflected in both ancient law and lore, attesting to the polygamous family being perennially threatened by the potential disruption of its hierarchy of women, be they bona fide wives or concubines.

12. Lev. 18:18: וְאִשָּׁה אֶל־אֲחֹתָהּ לֹא תִקָּח לִצְרֹר לְגַלּוֹת עֶרְוָתָהּ עָלֶיהָ בְּחַיֶּיהָ

> Do not take/marry a woman as a rival to her sister, uncovering her nakedness during her [the sister's] lifetime.

13. 1 Sam. 1:6.

14. On David's succession and Bathsheba's involvement, in particular, see 1 Kings 1:5–31 and 2:13–25.

15. Current websites contain lists of a wide array of genders—for example, "What Are the 72 Other Genders?" (Allarakha n.d.) and "57 Genders (and None for Me?)—Part Two" (Barker n.d.). I have not included intersex here because intersex is not a gender identity. Intersex people have the same variety of gender identities and sexual orientations that people born biologically male or female do.

In the field of biblical studies, gender identity has been explored in a variety of recent sources, including Katherine Apostolacus, "The Bible and The Transgender Christian: Mapping Transgender Hermeneutics in the 21st Century," *Journal of the Bible and its Reception* 5, no. 1 (2018): 1–29; Samuel Ross, "A Transgender Gaze at Genesis 38," *Journal for Interdisciplinary Biblical Studies* 2, no. 1 (2020): 25–29; Ayasha W. Musa, "Jael Is Non-binary; Jael Is Not a Woman," *Journal of Interdisciplinary Studies* 2, no. 1 (2020): 97–120; S. Cornwall, ed., *Intersex, Theology, and the Bible: Troubling Bodies in Church, Text, and Society* (Palgrave Macmillan, 2016).

16. M. L. Haupert, Amanda N. Gesselman, Amy C. Moors, Helen E. Fisher, and Justin R. Garcia, "Prevalence of Experiences with Consensual Nonmonogamous Relationships: Findings from Two National Samples of Single Americans," *Journal of Sex & Marital Therapy* 43, no. 5 (2017): 426 ("Men and sexual minorities were more likely to report current engagement in a CNM [consensual non-monogamous] relationship"). Also see "Sexual and Gender Orientation" (427–28) for a more detailed discussion.

17. Christina Richards, "Trans and Non-Monogamies," in *Understanding Non-Monogamies*, edited by Meg Barker and Darren Langdridge (New York: Routledge, 2009), 132.

18. Richards, "Trans and Non-Monogamies," 129.

19. Some exceptions to this assumption may be found in the ways, for example, that the classical rabbis described certain biblical characters in the midrash, such as in Genesis Rabbah 84:7, where Joseph is described as "doing youthful things. He touched up his eyes, he picked up his heels, he fixed his hair." Although they do not overtly say that he is homosexual, this type of description may be understood as implying that (albeit in a fairly stereotypical fashion). See M. Carden, "Genesis/Bereshit," in *The Queer Bible Commentary*, edited by Deryn Guest, Robert E. Goss, Mona West, and Thomas Bohache (London: SCM Press, 2015), 21–60. In particular, Carden writes, "Twirling, mincing, in rainbow garb with painted eyes, Joseph is a flaming young queen" (53). Also see Deryn Guest, "Troubling the Waters: תהום, Transgender, and Reading Genesis Backwards," in *Transgender, Intersex, and Biblical Interpretation*, edited by Teresa J. Hornsby and Deryn Guest (Atlanta: SBL, 2016), 47: "It [transgender engagement with biblical texts] could also involve work on biblical characters that appear to have trans significance or resonance, such as Joseph."

20. Works dealing with queer interpretations of a range of biblical characters and stories include, for example, Deryn Guest, Robert E. Goss, Mona West, and Thomas Bohache, eds., *The Queer Bible Commentary* (London: SCM Press, 2015); Ken Stone, *Queer Commentary and the Hebrew Bible* (London: Sheffield Phoenix Press, 2001); and Andrew Ramer, *Queering the Text: Biblical, Medieval, and Modern Jewish Stories* (Maple Shade, NJ: Lethe Press, 2010), to name but a few.

21. Jay Michaelson, "What Does the Bible Teach about Transgender People?" *The Daily Beast*, March 3, 2018.

22. Although some commentators suggest that Mordecai was waiting for Esther to be old enough to marry her himself, this idea is not at all clear from the text. If that were the case, why would he risk sending her to the king's "beauty contest," in which the most likely outcome would have been that she would be forced to have sex with the king once and then sent back to his harem, rendering her unmarriageable by anyone else?

23. See note 8 for the details of David's wives.

24. NJPS צַר־לִי עָלֶיךָ אָחִי יְהוֹנָתָן נָעַמְתָּ לִּי מְאֹד נִפְלְאַתָה אַהֲבָתְךָ לִי מֵאַהֲבַת נָשִׁים:

25. Stephen Greenberg, *Wresting with God and Men: Homosexuality in the Jewish Tradition* (Madison: University of Wisconsin Press, 2004), 103. For a fuller study, see J. E. Harding, *The Love of David and Jonathan: Ideology, Text, Reception* (Abingdon, Oxon: Taylor & Francis, 2016).

26. I want to acknowledge that terms such as "gender nonconforming," "bi-curious," and so on are clearly anachronistic in the context of the Hebrew Bible, but just because the ancient world did not use this terminology does not mean that people did not experience their gender and sexuality in complex and diverse ways, just as people have done throughout history and continue to do so today. Furthermore, and for the alleviation of doubt, as with the whole of this book, I am not suggesting that David was "really" bisexual or that Jacob was "really" gender nonconforming, or that Mordecai was "really" asexual. Rather, I am asking what happens if we examine the possible textual clues to read them this way and explore the new avenues of interpretation that open up from such readings.

27. Chris McKnight, "Polygamy and the Problem of Patriarchy," *Patheos.com*, November 7, 2017.

28. McKnight, "Polygamy and the Problem of Patriarchy." In point 5, McKnight includes the concept of consent. As I will discuss in chapter 8 of this book, the subject of consent is problematic when applied to the heteropatriarchal world of the Hebrew Bible. McKnight's point speaks to a contemporary understanding of consent within sexual and/or marital relationships. In applying McKnight's framework to the biblical world, I will be looking, therefore, for clues that can point us, as readers, toward the degree to which the characters are able to make active choices about what happens to them and can, thereby, consent to that course of action.

29. There are no examples of polyandrous (or any other sort of overt polyamorous) relationships in the Hebrew Bible, so when reading the Hebrew Bible, we are forced to differentiate only among the polygamous relationships described. Clearly, most (if not all) of the examples I detailed previously would fall into the category of patriarchal polygamy.

30. Polyfidelity is certainly not the only form of polyamory practiced in contemporary times, nor am I advocating for polyfidelity as a preferred model for polyamory. Indeed, Jessica Fern outlines at least ten different versions of polyamory, including "monogamish," "relationship anarchy," "poly-intimates," and so forth. Jessica Fern, *Polysecure: Attachment, Trauma and Consensual Nonmonogamy* (Portland, OR: Thorntree Press, 2020), 110.

31. Fern, *Polysecure*, 111: "Polyfidelity: A romantic or sexual relationship that involves more than two people, but these people are exclusive with each other. This could include a group relationship of three or more people that is closed to any additional outside partners."

Also see, for example, https://bisexuality.fandom.com/wiki/Polyfidelity.

32. Cf. Jin Haritaworn, Chin-ju Lin, and Christian Klesse, "Poly/logue: A Critical Introduction to Polyamory," *Sexualities* 9, no. 5 (2006): 515–29.

33. For a powerful refutation of anachronism arguments in biblical studies, see Barbara Thiede, *Rape Culture in the House of David* (Abingdon, Oxon: Routledge, 2022), 3–8, discussing the use of the term "rape culture" in reference to the Hebrew Bible.

34. Again, as I have explained previously, I would include many (if not most) polygamous relationships in the Hebrew Bible as McKnight's "patriarchal polygamy."

35. See note 28.

36. Deryn Guest, *When Deborah Met Jael: Lesbian Biblical Hermeneutics* (London: SCM Press, 2005), 110.

37. Guest, *When Deborah Met Jael*, 124. See Elisabeth Schüssler Fiorenza, *Bread Not Stone: The Challenge of Feminist Biblical Interpretation* (Boston: Beacon Press, 1984), for more on the feminist hermeneutic of suspicion.

38. Guest, *When Deborah Met Jael*, 124.

39. Guest, *When Deborah Met Jael*, 124 (italics original).

40. Guest, *When Deborah Met Jael*, 159 (italics original).

41. Guest, *When Deborah Met Jael*, 159.

42. Guest, *When Deborah Met Jael*, 159.

43. Guest, *When Deborah Met Jael*, 159.

44. I do want to emphasize and clarify that I am discussing theory here rather than, necessarily, lived experience. As Rabbi Nikki DeBlosi has pointed out to me in personal correspondence, "while our poly relationships might challenge gender binaries and destabilize them in the way that gender as a repeated performance always allows for the exposure of (and reversal of) a gender hierarchy and binary, embodied people still live under a sexist gender binary."

45. Guest, *When Deborah Met Jael*, 209.

46. Guest, *When Deborah Met Jael*, 239.

47. Cf. Rabbi Nikki DeBlosi, "Toward a New Framework for Reform Jewish Views on Polyamory," *Reform Jewish Quarterly* (Fall 2022): 76–92.

48. Additionally, "they have been pushed to the margins, discriminated against, maligned, misrepresented, mocked, erased and actively excluded—including in law and popular culture" (Johanna Steibert, personal correspondence).

49. In particular, I would like to thank the attendees at the Gender, Sexuality, and the Bible section of the SBL Annual Meeting 2021, who were so encouraging about my work and understood immediately how important this topic might be to people living polyamorous lives.

50. And, I hope, beyond and more widely in societies in which the text of the Hebrew Bible and its interpretation, even among more secular populations, play a role in public discourse and in creating cultural norms.

51. Barry Holtz, *Back to the Sources: Reading the Classic Jewish Texts* (New York: Simon & Schuster, 1984), 16–17 (italics original).

52. The SBL academic transliteration is *dābār ʾaḥēr*; however, I will use the more common transliteration of *davar acher*.

53. Yitzhak Franks, *The Practical Talmud Dictionary* (Jerusalem: Ariel United Israel Institutes, 1991), 65.

54. Midrashic polysemy, certainly in an antiquity, was not completely without boundaries. The rabbis created a long list of *middot* (rabbinic hermeneutics) for creating midrashic interpretations. See Gunter Stemberger, *Introduction to the Talmud and Midrash* (Edinburgh: T&T Clark, 1991), 15–30, for an introduction to rabbinic hermeneutics, including the complete lists of these hermeneutics.

55. The original source of this midrash is in Seder Olam Rabbah 21, where the proof texts are listed without any explanatory commentary. In this repetition of the midrash, the rabbis have explicated the proof texts.

56. Marcus Jastrow, *Dictionary of the Targumim, Talmud Bavli, Talmud Yerushalmi and Midrashic Literature* (Judaica Treasury, 1871), 989.

57. Tannaitic literature refers to the literature produced by the early strand of rabbinic sages, the *Tannaim*, who date to the first two centuries of the Common Era.

58. Rabbi Adin Steinsaltz, *The Talmud: The Steinsaltz Edition—A Reference Guide* (New York: Random House, 1989), 109.

59. For examples of some of the many other ways of reading the Book of Ruth, see the following: Rachel E. Adelman, *The Female Ruse: Women's Deception & Divine Sanction in the Hebrew Bible* (Sheffield: Sheffield Phoenix Press, 2017), 90–125; Rebekah Alpert, "Finding Our Past: A Lesbian Interpretation of the Book of Ruth," in *Reading Ruth: Contemporary Women Reclaim a Sacred Story*, edited

by Judith A. Kates and Gail Twersky Reimer (New York: Ballantine Books, 1996), 91–96; Julie Li-Chuan Chu, "Returning Home: The Inspiration of the Role Differentiation in the Book of Ruth for Taiwanese Women," in *Reading the Bible as Women: Perspectives from Africa, Asia, and Latin America* (Semeia 78), edited by Katherine Doob Sakenfeld and Sharon H. Ringe (Atlanta: SBL, 1997), 47–53; Celena M. Duncan, "The Book of Ruth: On Boundaries, Love, and Truth," in *Take Back the Word: A Queer Reading of the Bible*, edited by Robert E. Goss and Mona West (Cleveland, OH: Pilgrim Press, 2000), 92–102; Laura E. Donaldson, "The Sign of Orpah: Reading Ruth through Native Eyes," in *A Feminist Companion to the Bible: Ruth and Esther (Second Series)*, edited by Athayla Brenner (Sheffield: Sheffield Academic Press, 1999), 130–44; Irmtraud Fischer, "The Book of Ruth as Exegetical Literature," *European Judaism: A Journal for the New Europe* 40, no. 2 (2007): 140–49; Edward L. Greenstein, "Reading Strategies and the Story of Ruth," in *Women in the Hebrew Bible*, edited by Alice Bach (New York: Routledge, 1999), 211–31; André Lacocque, *The Feminine Unconventional: Four Subversive Figures in Israel's Tradition* (Eugene, OR: Wipf & Stock, 2005), 84–116; Madipoane Masenya, "Ruth," in *Global Bible Commentary*, edited by Daniel Patte (Nashville: Abingdon Press, 2004), 86–92; Judith E. McKinley, *Reframing Her: Biblical Women in Postcolonial Focus* (Sheffield: Sheffield Phoenix Press, 2004), particularly chapter 3, "Reading Ruth and Rahab" (37-56); Ellen van Wolde, "Intertextuality: Ruth in Dialogue with Tamar," in *A Feminist Companion to Reading the Bible: Approaches, Methods and Strategies*, edited by Athalya Brenner and Carole Fontaine (Sheffield: Sheffield Academic Press, 1997), 426–51; and Gale A. Yee, "'She Stood in Tears Amid the Alien Corn': Ruth, the Perpetual Foreigner and Model Minority," in *They Were All Together in One Place? Toward Minority Biblical Criticism*, edited by Randall C. Bailey, Tat-siong Benny Liew, and Fernando F. Segovia (Atlanta: SBL, 2009), 119–40. See also Gafney, "Mother Knows Best," 23–36.

60. Louis Jacobs, *The Jewish Religion: A Companion* (Oxford: Oxford University Press, 1995), 535; Étan Levine, *The Aramaic Version of the Bible: Contents and Context* (Berlin: de Gruyter, 1988), 11–13.

61. The exception is in Yemenite communities, where the reading aloud of the Targum has continued into modern times. I use the term *progressive* as it is employed by the largest grouping of Jews internationally, the World Union of Progressive Judaism (www.wupj.org).

62. Leonard Greenspoon, "Jewish Translations of the Bible," in *The Jewish Study Bible*, edited by Adele Berlin and Marc Zvi Brettler (Oxford: Oxford University Press, 2004), 2008.

63. Levine, *The Aramaic Version of the Bible*, 14.

64. For examples of contemporary feminist midrash, see Naomi Graetz, *Unlocking the Garden: A Feminist Jewish Look at the Bible, Midrash and God* (Piscataway, NJ: Gorgias Press, 2005), and Tamar Biala, ed., *Dirshuni: Contemporary Women's Midrash* (Waltham, MA: Brandeis University Press, 2022).

65. הַמְתַרְגֵּם פָּסוּק כְּצוּרָתוֹ הֲרֵי זֶה בַּדַּאי וְהַמּוֹסִיף עָלָיו הֲרֵי זֶה מְחָרֵף

66. And offering the possibility for a community to incorporate my reading into liturgical usage.

Chapter 1

The Setting

Ruth 1 begins simply—deceptively so. Verse 1 opens by situating the story: וַיְהִי בִּימֵי שְׁפֹט הַשֹּׁפְטִים, "It happened in the time that the judges judged." But already, even these first four words have major significance.

In the case of the Old Testament as well as the Septuagint, this opening has determined where the Book of Ruth ought to be located within the order of the biblical canon. The Book of Ruth, much like the eponymous character herself, is somewhat peripatetic. Though in the Old Testament the Book of Ruth is always found after Judges, in the Hebrew Bible it is found among the Writings (*Ketuvim*), the third and final section of the Hebrew Bible.[1] According to *B. Baba Batra* 14b, Ruth is the first book of *Ketuvim* based on the chronological ordering of the books according to the ascription of authorship.[2] By the late ninth century, the order had changed in favor of placing Ruth among the *Megillot*, where it is to be found in contemporary Hebrew Bibles, albeit with the order among the constituent books of the *Megillot* themselves having shifted over time to reflect current liturgical usage.[3]

What is crucial about Ruth's location is context. Does Ruth follow on from the Book of Judges as a sort of pastoral interlude between the blood and guts of intertribal warfare and the establishment of orderly monarchic rule, or does the reference to the time of the judges function more like the fairy tale opening "once upon a time"? Should we read Ruth between multiple stories of gender-based violence and misogyny—the brutal rape and murder of the Levite's secondary wife, which will ultimately lead to the rape-marriage of a large number of Israelite women (Judg. 19–21), and the story of Hannah, barren and unhappy, tormented by her rival, Peninnah, and falsely accused of inebriation by the priest, Eli (1 Sam. 1)? Or should we read Ruth between the highly emotionally charged voices of women in the *Megillot*—the empowered but frustrated voice of the female lover in the Song of Songs and the traumatized but challenging voice of Zion in Lamentations? Or ought we to read Ruth between the stories of two empowered women, the חַיִל אֵשֶׁת (*eshet hayil*) of Proverbs 31 (the very same term is used regarding Ruth herself in Ruth 3:11) and the aforementioned female lover of Song of Songs?[4]

Looking first at the Book of Judges, it contains numerous stories that share multiple common features: lawlessness and brutality, upending of normative gender and class roles, lack of unified leadership, and intertribal warfare. Judges is the "Wild West" of the Hebrew Bible—an unsettled period in which the previous constraints of society have been loosened as the new, settled community is being formed. Judges tells the stories of a range of curious figures: for example, an illegitimately born, uneducated leader; a female leader who commands men; and a divinely foretold leader who is nevertheless brought down by a wily, foreign woman.[5] If the story of Ruth takes place during this time in Israelite history, then the reader is being clued in that normal rules do not apply. The reader is thus granted a heads-up; what follows will *not* be as expected. Anything goes and much more when we find ourselves in the time of the judges. Whether the Book of Ruth is located immediately following Judges is not pertinent here; it is the *setting* during the time when "the judges judged," this liminal moment in Israelite history, that warns readers of what to expect—namely, another liminal story that doesn't quite follow the rules.

But what about the canonical context? Which stories and which women should we consider the character Ruth's reference points—following the Levite's secondary wife and the women of Shiloh and preceding Hannah and Peninnah? Following the female lover of the Song of Songs and preceding the voice of the female personified figure of Zion? Following the woman of valor in Proverbs and preceding the female lover of the Song? Reading Ruth immediately following on from Judges 21 helps Wil Gafney, for example, make a case for reading Ruth's marriage to Mahlon as a rape-marriage.[6] Gafney's reading is based on linguistic similarity with the story of the rape-marriage of the women of Shiloh, which, in turn, supports Gafney's larger framework of reading the figure of Ruth as a woman subjected to "sexploitation" by her mother-in-law, who goes on to use Ruth as her surrogate (albeit potentially willingly) to produce the birth of a son.[7]

Although Gafney does not discuss the story of Hannah that follows Ruth in the Old Testament, reading the story of Ruth between these reference points directs the reader to stories of fertility, progeny, and patriarchy. The men of Benjamin in Judges 21 "require" wives so that their tribal line will not die out. Both the women of Jabesh-gilead and those of Shiloh, who are kidnapped and raped into marriage, are nameless pawns in the patriarchal game of intertribal warfare. Conversely, Hannah is loved by her husband but taunted by her fertile co-wife, Peninnah, when Hannah cannot become pregnant. Her eventual progeny is, like Ruth's, never primarily her son; rather, he is Eli's protégé, the prophet Samuel, who becomes the central figure in the establishment of the male-dominated monarchy of Israel. Whether loved or not, happily married or not, all of these women are necessary for their procreative abilities and nothing much else. Reading Ruth among them could help underpin a reading of the book as focused primarily on Ruth's procreative abilities with, perhaps, only a sideline in considering how a heteronormative romance might develop within the constraints of the patriarchal system stemming from the period of the judges.

Reading Ruth between the female lover of the Song of Songs and the person-ification of Zion in Lamentations, however, grants us different insights into her character. Both the female lover and Zion have strong voices that give insight into their emotional lives.[8] Both figures are highly passionate, confronting the reader with the full force of their inner turmoil and distress at the situations in which they find themselves. The female lover expresses her desire for her beloved in highly explicit language, sometimes to the point of desperation. Her voice is clear, and her expression of her desire is much less bounded by patriar-chy than almost any other female voice in the Hebrew Bible.[9] In this sense, she is a challenge to the patriarchal system in which she lives. Zion's voice, too, is clear in expressing her pain and suffering at the hands of men and God.[10] She rails against the violence wrought against her and perhaps especially against this situation being cast as punishment for sin, which in turn presents a pro-found, gender-based, theological challenge to Israel's covenantal relationship with God. Both the female lover's and Zion's voices present real challenges to the social norms of patriarchy as described across the Hebrew Bible. Reading Ruth in *this* context might suggest that Ruth, too, is the owner of a powerful, passionate voice, who is not afraid to challenge patriarchal norms.

Reading Ruth in the context of the *eshet hayil* of Proverbs provides a model for Ruth as a flawless woman. The end of the Book of Proverbs (Prov. 31:10–31) describes this idealized woman. She spins and weaves, provides provisions for her family, plants vineyards, engages in mercantile business, provides for the poor, clothes herself and her family, sleeps very little, and ensures that her husband can sit at the gates of the city. She bears children, is wise and full of *hesed*, is never idle, and, most important, is God-fearing. In short, she is the perfect, pious superwoman.[11] Both the allusion to Ruth as an *eshet hayil* and the three key references to *hesed* in the Book of Ruth make for a strong intertextual reading of this Proverbs passage.[12] If we read Ruth between the *eshet hayil* and the female lover of the Song, Ruth becomes not only the perfect helpmate for any husband but also one who is capable of being vocally passionately in love. Ruth, in this context, is neither subor-dinated nor empowered; she is, perhaps, more Stepford Wife than anything else.

So, the context for reading Ruth matters. It can help reinforce stereotypes or break them down. But knowing that as readers we start from a point of carrying certain baggage, certain expectations of Ruth herself (indeed, likely all of the other characters, too) can help us break down our barriers to other potential readings.

NOTES

1. Judges, by comparison, is the second book of the second section of the Hebrew Bible, Prophets (*Nevi'im*).

2. The order of the writings: Ruth and the Book of Psalms, Job and Proverbs, Ecclesiastes, Song of Songs and Lamentations, Daniel and the Scroll of Esther, Ezra and Chronicles.

סִידְרָן שֶׁל כְּתוּבִים רוּת וְסֵפֶר תְּהִלִּים וְאִיּוֹב וּמִשְׁלֵי קֹהֶלֶת שִׁיר הַשִּׁירִים וְקִינוֹת דָּנִיאֵל וּמְגִילַת אֶסְתֵּר אֶזְרָא וְדִבְרֵי הַיָּמִים

The passage goes on to explain that Samuel wrote the Book of Ruth and Judges. The rabbis also acknowledge that Job was written before Ruth and attempt to justify the order here by appealing to Ruth's happy ending as a more appropriate way to begin.

3. The term *Megillot* (scrolls) refers to the following five books (in their current festival order in a Hebrew Bible): Song of Songs, Ruth, Lamentations, Ecclesiastes, and Esther.

The original Masoretic ordering of the *Megillot* is as follows: Ruth, Song of Songs, Ecclesiastes, Lamentations, and Esther.

For a fuller discussion of the development of the order of the Writings (and Ruth in particular) in the Hebrew Bible, see Timothy Stone, *A Compilation History of the Megilloth* (Tübingen: Mohr Siebeck, 2013), 79–117.

4. Prov. 31:10–31. Translated variously as "woman of valor" (JPS 1917), "capable wife" (NJPS/NRSV), "virtuous woman" (KJV), and "wife of noble character" (NIV).

Another option, from the original Talmudic order, would be to read Ruth between the end of *Nevi'im*, which is Malachi, and the Book of Psalms, which I have not discussed here.

5. Jephthah, Deborah, and Samson, respectively.

6. Gafney, "Mother Knows Best," 26–30.

7. Gafney, "Mother Knows Best," 30–32 and 34–35.

8. Of course, so does Hannah. The women at the end of the Book of Judges have no voice at all.

9. Though even her voice is constrained by the reality of living in a society in which men—her brothers, for example—have power over her. According to Clines,

> She is a strange one, this woman in the Song of Songs. She is, literally, a strange woman, an *'ishshah zarah*—and that is because she does not exist. She is not a real woman, she is a figment of the poet's imagination. What's more, she is his wish-fulfilment dream. He dreams her up precisely because she does not exist.

David Clines, "Why Is There a Song of Songs and What Does It Do to You If You Read It?" in *Interested Parties: The Ideology of Writers and Readers of the Hebrew Bible* (Sheffield: Sheffield Academic Press, 1995), 107.

10. See Carleen Mandolfo's groundbreaking work on the subject for a full treatment of this subject. Carleen R. Mandolfo, *Daughter Zion Talks Back to the Prophets: A Dialogic Theology of the Book of Lamentations* (Atlanta: SBL, 2007).

11. For reading that "can offer partially liberating possibilities," of the *eshet hayil*, see Madipoane Masenya's "Proverbs 31:10–31 in a South African Context: A Reading for the Liberation of African (Northern Sotho) Women," in *Reading the Bible as Women: Perspectives from Africa, Asia, and Latin America* (Semeia 78), edited by Katherine Doob Sakenfeld and Sharon H. Ringe (Atlanta: SBL, 1997), 55–68.

12. Cf. Laura Quick, "Ruth and the Limits of Proverbial Wisdom Author(s)," *Journal of Biblical Literature* 139, no. 1 (2020), 61–62; Gale A. Yee, "'She Stood in Tears Amid the Alien Corn': Ruth, the Perpetual Foreigner and Model Minority," in *They Were All Together in One Place? Toward Minority Biblical Criticism*, edited by Randall C. Bailey, Tat-siong Benny Liew, and Fernando F. Segovia (Atlanta: SBL, 2009), 119–40.

Chapter 2

Ruth 1

The Arrangement and Rearrangement of Families

FROM QUAD TO TRIAD (RUTH 1:1–6)

Beyond the scene setting, Ruth 1 introduces the reader to a range of different family configurations. At the outset of the story, Ruth 1:1 tells of "a man, his wife, and two sons," who are not named until the following verse. They are simply the most basic form of family that every reader will surely recognize—a standard, heteronormative, nuclear family.[1] They are described as though they are paper doll cutouts, just waiting to be clothed with the reader's imagination. But verse 2 fleshes them out, gives clues in the form of their names as to who they might be and become. Elimelech, the father, means "God is my king"; Naomi, the mother, "kindness of God"; and Mahlon and Chilion, the sons, "sickness" and "destruction," respectively.[2] The parents are pious and kind, but the sons do not seem destined for long, prosperous lives.

So for two whole verses, the text presents this basic family unit as they journey from their home in Bethlehem to Moab in order to find food during a period of drought. But as soon as they arrive in verse 3, the family takes on a new configuration, for Elimelech, whom the text explicitly states is Naomi's husband (as though the reader did not know this information already), dies at the beginning of the verse. A curious inversion is taking place here. In verse 1, Naomi is possessed by her husband, but here in verse 3, the tables are turned. The dead Elimelech belongs to Naomi, but dead husbands are of no use in ancient Israel. Yet now the two sons also belong to Naomi, and again the text explicitly tells the reader so. What will happen to this new family—a widow with two sons?

So in the third formation of the family in a mere four verses, Naomi's two sons "lift up" wives for themselves from among the Moabites—Orpah and

Ruth.[3] This third family unit—Naomi, her two sons, and her two daughters-in-law—have resided together in Moab for about ten years, a situation that appears to be stable and unchanging, much to the surprise of anyone who understands the purpose of marriage in the Hebrew Bible. Yet the text does not state that either Orpah or Ruth is infertile, which might be expected from our knowledge of how other biblical stories work, such as Sarah and Abraham, Rebekah and Isaac, Rachel and Jacob, or Hannah and Elkanah. Clearly, "sickness" and "destruction" (Mahlon and Chilion) were never going to be fertile anyway. This story is not, after all, their tale, but neither is it the straightforward, more common plot of female infertility.

Verse 5 presents yet another family unit, for Mahlon and Chilion die at the beginning of the verse, leaving "the woman" without either her sons or her husband. The focus of the text is on "the woman," not Naomi, as if, in losing both her sons and her husband, she is back to being that cardboard cutout of verse 1. Who is this "woman" without the surround of family? What happens to a woman who has fulfilled all of the required functions of womanhood in patriarchal, biblical society—marriage and bearing children, particularly sons—and then loses them all? She goes from having a name to being nameless. As she begins her move (verse 6) with her similarly generically identified "daughters-in-law," she will remain unnamed until verse 8.

Alternatively, perhaps the text must refer to her as a "woman" because it might not otherwise be obvious what Naomi was. Being widowed and having deceased sons, who left no progeny, makes Naomi difficult to classify. As the text will relate later (verse 12), Naomi is past childbearing years as well. She has tried and failed in her central role as a woman in ancient Israel. What should her identity be now? Does the emphasis on her as a "woman" serve to remind the reader that she is still female, lest we think that some other option might be available to her now?

But despite the reporting in verse 5, Naomi is not alone. She has another family configuration of sorts, one that will spark more dialog than any of the ones that have preceded it (indeed, no dialog has occurred at all yet in the story). Naomi, Orpah, and Ruth continue to reside together, bound to each other in their widowhoods. This reality is not even alluded to in verse 5; it must be derived from context. Only in verse 6 does the text remind us that "she" is not actually alone.

Table 2.1 highlights a number of points:

• The majority of family units in these verses are atypical of the biblical ideal. (Only in verses 1–2 is there a typical patriarchal family unit.)
• These family units progress from predominantly male units to predominantly female units.

- The family units in these opening verses contain familiar models, less familiar models, and models without any other referent in the Hebrew Bible.
- The changing family units progress very quickly during these opening verses.

Table 2.1 Family Units in Ruth 1:1–6

Verse	Family Unit
1–2	Man, woman, two sons
3	Woman, two sons
4	Woman, two sons + two daughters-in-law
5	One woman*
6	Three women*

*Notably without children, particularly without sons.

Perhaps the starkest issue of all to note is that the day-to-day life of these family units is not described or commented on at all. Between verses 4 and 5, a period of some ten years elapses, and the reader knows nothing at all about how the lives of Naomi, Mahlon, Chilion, Orpah, and Ruth were organized and lived or why neither marriage produced surviving children. This missing ten years is a major lacuna in the text, which opens the way for imaginative questioning. How did the family survive? What work did each member do? Why were both couples childless? Are the archetypes portrayed by the names "sickness" and "destruction" enough to explain the childlessness? But if so, then why did Orpah and Ruth marry into the family at all?[4] What are the emotional relationships of the members of this family unit to each other? How did they encounter each other on a daily basis? What contact did these family members have with their neighbors? In short, how did they live, and what bonds developed between them?

Into this imaginative gap, Rabbi Beivai states in the name of the Rabbi Reuben that "Ruth and Orpah were the daughters of Eglon."[5] But this information tells us more about the concerns of the rabbis—namely, that King David should have some sort of royal lineage—than anything about the questions raised previously. It does suggest, however, that Ruth and Orpah are sisters, though no textual evidence at all exists to support this notion. What would it mean if they were sisters? Would that relationship help begin to answer the question about the emotional relationships of the various family members?[6]

Ruth 4:11 makes an intertextual allusion to the archetypal biblical sisters, Rachel and Leah. The people ask that Ruth be made like "Rachel and Leah, the two of whom built up the House of Israel." But Leah and Rachel did so as fierce competitors for the affection of the same husband within an

endogamous and polygamous marriage. Orpah and Ruth are not married
to the same man, though they do reside in the same larger household, and
they are both in exogamous marriages. Might these differences have created
the conditions for Orpah and Ruth to have a different sort of relationship
than Leah and Rachel? Might two women, whether sisters or not, who have
resided in the same household for ten years and appear to live under the same
conditions, both being childless, have developed a relationship not of competition but of support with each other? Might Ruth and Orpah be an inversion
of Rachel and Leah?[7]

TRIAD 1: RUTH–NAOMI–ORPAH (RUTH 1:6–14)

What about the relationship of Ruth and Orpah to Naomi as their mother-in-
law? The Hebrew Bible contains little (if any) meaningful narrative information about the relationship between mothers-in-law and daughters-in-law. In
fact, the only other verse to explicitly mention the relationship of daughters-
in-law to mothers-in-law in the Hebrew Bible is Mic. 7:6, which does so in
the context of a household out of kilter, where family members have turned
against each other as well as the patriarch.[8] The only thing to be gleaned
from this verse is that apparently mothers-in-law and daughters-in-law being
in conflict with each other is the exception, unlike the contemporary Western
stereotype of fraught relationships between the two. That being the case, we
might reasonably posit that Ruth, Orpah, and Naomi would have actually
striven to create a harmonious and supportive relationship with one another,
not only in adversity once they were all widowed but also long before then—
from the time the two women married into Naomi's household.

During the course of the ten years that Ruth and Orpah were married before
their husbands' deaths, they might have developed strong bonds to each other
and to Naomi. What would those years have been like? Though it is possible
that both Mahlon and Chilion simply died unexpectedly on the same day (or
at least within a short time of each other), equally possible is the idea that
both Mahlon and Chilion were ill for more extended periods of time, requir-
ing caring responsibilities from all three women. Setting up rotas for the care
of the sick while also keeping a household fed, clothed, and sheltered could
have created a tight-knit unit of the three women to ensure that all stayed
healthy and capable. They may have learned to rely on one another, not only
in day-to-day tasks but also emotionally.

Additionally, we know that Elimelech moved the family initially because
of famine. But when Naomi decides to leave Moab, her rationale is that she
has heard there is now food in Bethlehem. Could we infer that Moab is not
quite the land of plenty that Elimelech had imagined? Perhaps the women

were barely more than subsisting in Moab. That, too, would have bound them closer together as they worked to ensure that none of them starved.

But aside from the potentially difficult ten years that the text states the women spent together while their husbands/sons still lived, the text does not inform the reader of how many years passed between verses 5 and 6. The story reads almost as though one day Mahlon and Chilion died, and the next day Naomi decided to depart for Bethlehem. Although this reading is certainly possible, even just the planning for such a journey would likely have taken a certain amount of time. More likely is that the decision to depart for Bethlehem was one that took time to unfold.

So what did the relationship between Naomi, Orpah, and Ruth look like during this period? Marc Chagall's lithograph *Naomi, Ruth, and Orpah* depicts the three women during this period. His visual representation serves as a useful metatext for thinking through the women's relationship to each other.[9] Standing, huddled tightly together, all three figures appear female, with long dresses and long hair; moreover, the central figure is depicted with breasts. Presumably, the central figure is Naomi, flanked on either side by an in-profile daughter-in-law, but determining which of the two figures is Ruth or Orpah is more challenging. As one looks at the lithograph, the figure on the right has her eye open with her hand lying just below Naomi's breast. She looks alert, the arch of her eyebrow connoting desire, concern, or anguish—it is hard to know which precisely. The figure on the left has her eye closed and appears to be asleep (or at least resting on Naomi's shoulder). Her arm is merged completely into Naomi's body, so that the precise placement of her hand is impossible to determine. Naomi herself is open-eyed, staring entirely forward at the viewer, not gazing at all at either daughter-in-law, though her head is tilted toward the woman on the right, on whom she rests the side of her head. Naomi's hands are joined together, held in front of her lower abdomen. One of Naomi's uncovered feet protrudes from under her dress into the bottom center of the illustration. The other two women have uncovered feet as well, though they are harder to discern as they meld into the background. The three women, despite having distinct facial features, begin to blur together at their waistlines, where there are no lines at all separating them. Further down, the lines of Naomi's dress demarcate a boundary, again between the lower halves of their bodies.

The background itself is fairly plain: a few bushes, and in the lower left-hand corner there is the front half of a small lamb. In the top right-hand corner is the only brightly colored object in the work—two semi-circles of red-orange blurred into a pinkish-white mark out the sun. The rest of the lithograph consists of thin, precise black lines and washed-out, greyer-toned, thicker lines to mark out the objects against a background of muted shades of ochre.

Overall, the illustration is somewhat bleak but not maudlin. The subdued colors of the background against the fading warmth of the muffled sunlight, which does not penetrate beyond the top right corner, suggest quiet discomfort. Nothing in the women's appearance suggests hunger or deprivation, but neither do any of them look happy. The figure on the left is the most content of the three, able as she is to rest. The figure on the right is less content, more attentive. Naomi is, perhaps, resigned. They are only barely separated figures, nearly merging completely into each other.

So, who is content on Naomi's shoulder, and who reaches for her breast? What does each of these actions signify? Does the lamb in the bottom-left corner signify the sacrifice that one of these women will make? Is the sun setting on their comfortable relationship with one another? How would Naomi stand up, literally and metaphorically, if she did not have the support of her daughters-in-law? What binds the three of them so closely together that they nearly merge into a single figure? Is it possible for them to exist so comfortably without all three of them there?

What Chagall's illustration throws into sharp relief is the deep bond both Ruth and Orpah have clearly formed with Naomi. But where one of her daughters-in-law rests comfortably on her shoulder, the other lays her hand on Naomi's breast. The woman on the left displays something like a post-coital ease and total relaxation; in contrast, the woman on the right looks down toward the place of her hand just below Naomi's breast, her fingertips brushing the spot where Naomi's nipple would be. While not a depiction that at first blush appears overtly sexual, it is precisely the undercurrent of an allusion to something too taboo to be expressed openly, which draws me to the Chagall illustration. Could the same be said of Naomi, Orpah, and Ruth's relationship?

If we restrict ourselves to imagining that biblical characters must only ever act within the confines of patriarchal, heteronormative behaviors and structures, then Naomi, Ruth, and Orpah's relationship can never be anything more than that of three bereaved women mourning together for their deceased male relatives. They will always be stuck in the roles assigned to them by the patriarchal context of the Hebrew Bible. But this story is, to a very large extent, a women's story. Two of the three main characters are female. The women collectively speak more lines than the men across the whole of the book, and certainly in the first chapter, in which no man speaks at all.[10] The women are the dominant force, especially in Chapter 1. In those circumstances, can it be so difficult to imagine that the three women had developed an emotionally intimate relationship that may have included some sexual desires or even erotic relations as well? Naomi is widowed, and potentially neither Orpah nor Ruth is having any sort of sexual relations with their husbands (and certainly not after their deaths). All three women are still people with sexual desires and needs. Could we imagine that they took solace in each other or even that Ruth and Orpah preferred Naomi to the (apparently) impotent men in their lives?

At first, when Naomi decides to leave Moab, both Ruth and Orpah come with her. Why does she not simply demand from the outset that they stay behind? Why does she wait until partway through their journey to send them back? Why doesn't she tell them from the outset that they will never be able to remarry the sons that she, Naomi, cannot bear? Has she perhaps (conveniently) forgotten that Orpah and Ruth may well not be welcome in Bethlehem? Has she fallen into such a comfortable arrangement with Ruth and Orpah that it is only on the road back to Bethlehem that she remembers that Bethlehem will not be like their home on the plains of Moab? Are all three of them so intimately attached that they could not imagine going on without each other?

Nothing in the Book of Ruth describes anything at all about the lives of Orpah, Naomi, and Ruth as they lived together, either with Mahlon and Chilion or after their deaths. Only the readers' imaginations can fill in this particular blank. But in looking only at the dialog between the three of them as Naomi finally attempts to send them back to the houses of their mothers midway through their journey to Bethlehem, it would be easy to lose sight of the simple fact that the three of them did live together and shared some sort of bond.

Orpah is too often viewed instrumentally as nothing more than a foil to the character of Ruth. But adopting this view allows the text to reduce Orpah to a two-dimensional caricature. The text gives little detail to do much else, and yet from antiquity onward, her extremely modest role in this first chapter has been enough both to deride and to champion her.[11] Either way, commentators generally pit Orpah against Ruth. Ruth is faithful because she stayed, whereas Orpah is criticized because she did as Naomi asked and left. Orpah is a role model to native women who choose their matriarchal home cultures, unlike Ruth, who allowed herself to be co-opted by the colonializing, patriarchal power that Naomi represents.[12]

In pitting Ruth and Orpah against each other, what commentators fail to note is that the text presents a stable and caring triangular relationship between the three women. When Naomi tries to break up this relationship, both Ruth *and Orpah* are distressed. Rather than seeing Orpah as a useful device for showcasing Ruth's fidelity, we could instead see that her loss is a destabilizing feature in the relationship between Ruth and Naomi—a void that Naomi will try later to fill with Boaz (see chapter 3). The triangular Orpah-Naomi-Ruth relationship can foreshadow the importance of the tri-angular Boaz-Naomi-Ruth relationship. Viewed in this fashion, the Book of Ruth can be seen more broadly to foreground triangular relationships in a positive fashion, unlike any other book of the Hebrew Bible.

FROM TRIADS TO DYADS (RUTH 1:14–22)

וַתִּשֶּׂנָה קוֹלָן וַתִּבְכֶּינָה עוֹד וַתִּשַּׁק עָרְפָּה לַחֲמוֹתָהּ וְרוּת דָּבְקָה בָּהּ׃

14. They lifted up their voices and they cried more. Orpah kissed her mother-in-law, but Ruth clung to her.

At the beginning of verse 14, Orpah finally accedes to Naomi's request and departs for her mother's house in Moab. The stable triadic relationship that had been built up between the three women was dissolved with that act. But as Orpah leaves, she weeps—her leaving is not an easy act or decision—and then kisses her mother-in-law. The text does not describe this kiss, though clearly many different types of kiss exist. What sort of kiss did Orpah give Naomi? Only our imaginations can answer that question. The typically terse text gives no clues. Yet even the rabbis were clearly vexed by the question, as they felt the need to explicate in Ruth Rabbah 2:21:

> *Orpah kissed her mother-in-law.* All kissing is obscene,[13] except for three: A kiss of greatness, a kiss of having been separated, and a kiss of separation. A kiss of greatness, as it is written: "Samuel took a flask of oil, and poured it on his head, and kissed him" [1 Sam. 10:1].[14] Of having been separated, as it is written: "He met him at the mountain of God at Horev [and he kissed him]" [Exod. 4:27].[15] Of separation, as it is written: "Orpah kissed her mother-in-law." Rabbi Tanhuma said: Even a kiss of closeness,[16] as it is stated: "Jacob kissed Rachel" [Gen. 29:11]. Why? It is because she was his relative.[17]

The Hebrew Bible describes numerous acts of kissing, few of which have anything at all to do with eroticized behavior. Still, the fact that Orpah kisses Naomi must be explained away by the rabbis, lest the reader be in any doubt as to what sort of kiss it was. Below the surface of this kiss, however, might just be a hidden transcript breaking through.[18] After all, a kiss of departure, of what is sure to be permanent separation, might well look to all the world watching like an innocent gesture of filial devotion but may, even in its brief moment of enactment, convey far more—perhaps love, lust, passion, grief, or loss.

In the second half of the verse, however, before the reader can dwell too long on that kiss and before any question about Ruth's intention might be left hanging, straightaway we learn that Ruth does far more than remain with Naomi: דָּבְקָה בָּהּ (*dāḇəqāh bāh*), she clung to her. The use of the root ד.ב.ק. (*d .b.qh*) is intriguing. Scholars have debated the potential implications of the term, which in certain circumstances clearly has a sexual connotation but not in others. Jeremy Schipper summarizes the scholarship on the subject well, looking carefully not only at the root itself but also at the use of the inseparable prefix ב that follows here.[19] In such cases, the "context involves the attempted incorporation of a person into an Israelite household through marriage."[20] Yet a clear allusion to the use of this root remains in Gen. 2:24:

עַל־כֵּן יַעֲזָב־אִישׁ אֶת־אָבִיו וְאֶת־אִמּוֹ וְדָבַק בְּאִשְׁתּוֹ וְהָיוּ לְבָשָׂר אֶחָד׃

Therefore a man leaves his father and his mother and clings to his wife, and they become one flesh.

J. Cheryl Exum points out the potentially "unconscious heterosexist bias" of earlier male commentators in overlooking the "marriage-like quality" that the use of *dābǝqāh* may supply here.[21] Could *dābǝqāh* imply something more than "incorporation of a person into an Israelite household"? Does Ruth simply want to follow Naomi in the hopes of securing a new marriage in Bethlehem within the Israelite community, or is the use of *dābǝqāh* a deliberate intertextual reference to Gen. 2:24? If Ruth is intending to leave her family, cling to Naomi, and, by implication, become one flesh with her, then the text contains a not particularly well-hidden message of same-sex commitment between these two women.[22] If, as I have posited previously, Ruth, Naomi, and Orpah had already had a stable triadic relationship for a period of time, then Ruth's desire to continue to cling to Naomi makes even more sense. Perhaps Orpah cared for both Naomi and Ruth but was content to go home and find a more conventional relationship to sustain her, with her mother or a new husband, not fearing that she would be rejected by her natal Moabite family. Ruth, alternatively, could have feared returning to her family and/or had become so deeply committed to Naomi that she could not conceive of leaving her.

Nevertheless, whether *dābǝqāh* implies that Ruth and Naomi's relationship was of an erotic or sexual nature cannot be established definitively from the textual evidence alone, as Schipper points out:

To argue that the verb *dābaq* does not have a sexual or erotic implication in this verse does not discredit a queer reading of Ruth and Naomi's relationship unless one holds extremely reductive and mistaken ideas about queer identities. As with heterosexual desire, culturally conditioned expressions of queer desire include but are not limited to or solely defined by physical acts.[23]

What seems clear from the use of *dābǝqāh* is that the relationship between Ruth and Naomi is unique in some fashion—after all, the term is not employed in connection with any other unmarried women in the Hebrew Bible—and that the bond that Ruth feels with her mother-in-law is especially deep and committed.

The text could have expressed what happens between not only Ruth and Naomi but also Orpah and Naomi in a different fashion, but it does not. After all, verse 14 does not read, "They broke into weeping and Orpah returned to the house of her mother, while Ruth remained with her mother-in-law" (or something similar), which would have been a perfectly normal biblical way of expressing what might have happened. Instead, within the span of a mere six words, two highly charged terms are used—kissing and clinging. Listening carefully to these terms, we may find a hidden transcript of a different story being told about the nature of these women's relationships with one another.

Once the text has established that Ruth has clung to her mother-in-law, Naomi tries once more to get Ruth to leave. In verse 15, Naomi points out that Orpah has already left, returning to "her people and her gods." Ruth's reply in verses 16–17 is widely known and often quoted. If the reader had any doubt about Ruth's commitment to Naomi before this monologue, then no doubt is left afterward:

וַתֹּאמֶר רוּת אַל־תִּפְגְּעִי־בִי לְעָזְבֵךְ לָשׁוּב מֵאַחֲרָיִךְ כִּי אֶל־אֲשֶׁר תֵּלְכִי אֵלֵךְ וּבַאֲשֶׁר תָּלִינִי אָלִין עַמֵּךְ עַמִּי וֵאלֹהַיִךְ אֱלֹהָי: בַּאֲשֶׁר תָּמוּתִי אָמוּת וְשָׁם אֶקָּבֵר כֹּה יַעֲשֶׂה יְהוָה לִי וְכֹה יוֹסִיף כִּי הַמָּוֶת יַפְרִיד בֵּינִי וּבֵינֵךְ:

16. Ruth said, "Do not entreat me to abandon you to return from behind you [i.e., away from you] because wherever you go, I will go; and wherever you will rest overnight, I will rest overnight with you; your people, my people; and your God, my God.

17. Wherever you will die, I will die and there I will be buried. Thus the Eternal One will do to me and thus will add if death will cause a separation between me and you."

In these two verses, Ruth carefully crafts her response to Naomi in such a way that neither Naomi nor the reader can imagine Ruth being left behind to return to Moab. She asks Naomi to stop pleading with her, stressing that in Ruth's eyes, returning to the house of her mother in Moab would be an act of abandonment of Naomi. Ruth's personal bond to Naomi is simply too strong; she cannot leave her. Ruth never says why she feels that way, only that she does. Both Naomi and the reader must fill in the explanation and answer the *why* question left by the lacuna in Ruth's declaration.

Ruth goes on to say that wherever Naomi goes, she will go, and wherever Naomi rests overnight, that is where Ruth, too, will rest overnight. That makes sense in the context of the journey they are on. Ruth is committing herself to following Naomi, wherever Naomi's journey takes them. But Ruth is also committing to sleeping wherever Naomi sleeps. Of course, we can take this statement to mean that she will sleep in the same campsite or shelter that Naomi chooses, but, similar to the undercurrents potentially at play in verse 14, Ruth's desire to rest overnight with Naomi might hint at something more.

Next, Ruth responds directly to Naomi, who in verse 15 has entreated Ruth to return, as Orpah did, "to her people and to her gods." Ruth states clearly that her people are Naomi's people, and her God is Naomi's God. Ruth does not have any other people or gods, only Naomi's. In verse 15, Naomi does not yet appreciate the strength of Ruth's bond and commitment to her, but Ruth crafts her reply to address directly the issues Naomi raises.

Ruth does not stop once she has addressed these issues, however. Instead, she goes on to stress how full her desire is for integration into Naomi's life. In verse 17, she adds that wherever Naomi dies, that is where Ruth intends to die and be buried. Although she does not say so explicitly, the implication seems to be that she wishes to be buried alongside Naomi, much in the same way that married couples are buried within the same family compound.[24]

Ruth concludes by swearing an oath.[25] She is not merely expressing her feelings to Naomi but tying them up in a God-invoking vow. God may do to Ruth as God pleases and more, should anything that Ruth does cause her to be separated from Naomi. Ruth is most assuredly *not* returning to Moab or leaving Naomi behind. Ruth has left absolutely no doubt or way back from what she has said. An oath, once sworn, cannot be revoked easily.

Ruth does not mince her words here. She is terse, to the point, and clear and unequivocal about her actions. Her intentions are in no doubt, and yet she never explains or accounts for them. Ruth's motivation remains left to Naomi's and the reader's imagination. Taken in conjunction with *dābǝqāh* in verse 14, however, it is not hard to see that Ruth loves Naomi and that the type of love she feels is passionate, desirous, and committed. Ruth is, for all intents and purposes, what in modern English parlance would be described as "in love."[26]

But what of Naomi? Naomi's response—or, more accurately, her lack of response—gives the reader no clue. When Naomi sees Ruth's resolve, she simply stops arguing. Perhaps the older woman understands Ruth's feelings all too well, but she also knows what the social norms in Bethlehem are and determines that Ruth's feelings are irrelevant, whether or not Naomi reciprocates them. Perhaps Naomi believes that whatever life and whatever quality of relationship she has shared with Ruth (and Orpah) in Moab cannot be continued or replicated in Bethlehem.

Traditionally, the explanation given is that Naomi knew that a Moabitess would not be welcome in Bethlehem. While Naomi may have accepted her Moabite daughters-in-law into her family while they resided in Moab, Israelite territory would have been a different matter. Biblical law forbade marriage with Moabites, so Naomi's reluctance to let Ruth and Orpah return with her is obvious. But perhaps both things can be true: Naomi both recognizes her attachment to her daughters-in-law *and* realizes she cannot bring these two women, whom she loves (possibly in more than one fashion), back to Bethlehem. Perhaps only when faced with Ruth's utter determination is Naomi simply stunned, rendered speechless, into an acceptance that Ruth is capable of making her own life choices.

Finally, the chapter ends as the two women return to Bethlehem (although, in a literal sense, only Naomi actually returns). Now Naomi finally speaks, not to Ruth but to the women of Bethlehem whom they encounter. They hardly recognize Naomi. "Can this be Naomi?" they ask at the end of verse 19. Why don't they recognize her?

More than ten years during a period of famine and hardship change a person, including their appearance. But the women of Bethlehem know that the person they see before them is Naomi. If they did not, they would have asked something more like, "Who is this person we see before us?" They simply cannot entirely believe that the person they see is Naomi, perhaps because so many years have passed and they had not expected to see her again. Perhaps, too, Naomi is now postmenopausal. In verse 11, Naomi implies that she may well have passed her childbearing years, which would have brought about changes in her hormone levels. Postmenopausal women experience an array of physical changes, including (but not limited to) increased facial hair; receding hairlines; dry, flaking skin with decreased elasticity; increased weight gain with a redistribution of weight from the hip area to the central torso; changes in hair texture, often making hair frizzier; and so forth. Any of these changes could have made Naomi less recognizable to the women of Bethlehem and, indeed, could have also changed the way Naomi felt about her own body.

Maybe, though, their question reveals a hidden transcript breaking out. The women's question is vague enough to imply many things. To the patriarchally attuned biblical society listening, their question might have been taken at face value. But listened to another way, maybe something about Naomi's appearance is still familiar enough to be Naomi and different enough to be shockingly unrecognizable. What if, in traversing the road back with a young Moabitess in tow, Naomi had assumed the role of Ruth's husband, dressing in men's clothes to protect them from unwanted attentions?[27] What if Naomi, particularly in the period after her husband's death, took on characteristics conventionally regarded as masculine in order to lead her household, especially since neither of her sons might have been capable of doing so? Could these be the sorts of changes that the women of Jerusalem saw but could not entirely believe?

Whatever led to their question, Naomi's response confirms that she, too, believes she has changed. She tells them not to refer to her as Naomi anymore but as Mara, meaning "bitter." She explicates that this new name represents how she had left Bethlehem "full" (i.e., with the traditional heteropatriarchal family unit—in this case, a husband and two sons), and the Eternal One brought her back "empty" (i.e., without her husband or sons). The change that Naomi recognizes in herself is that she is no longer a part of the desired, normative structure of Israelite society, and she is bitter over that loss. We might consider that Naomi's acknowledgment of her bitterness at the loss of her social capital—that is, her heteropatriarchal family unit—negates her having any reciprocal feelings for Ruth, but this need not be the case.

Whatever Naomi's feelings may have been for Ruth, she would have been keenly aware that a husband and sons constituted social capital of a kind that Ruth, her Moabite, widowed daughter-in-law, could never match, not within the social value system of Bethlehem's community. Naomi could be mourning the loss of her status as much as (or, possibly, even more so than) Elimelech, Mahlon, and Chilion themselves.

In reaction to this change of status, she demands a change of name—one that is subsequently never used again by anyone in the rest of the story (including Naomi herself). Change of name is an important trope, both in the Hebrew Bible and in contemporary conversations about identity. Abram and Sarai became Abraham and Sarah after making a covenant with God. Subsequently, they are exclusively referred to by their new(ish) names.[28] Jacob is renamed Israel after he wrestles with the angel of God, though he is only rarely referred to as Israel thereafter in the text.[29] Both of these name changes happen after a positive, though strenuous, engagement with God. In the case of Abraham and Sarah, fertility is part of the promise that flows from their engagement which includes the change of their names. In the case of Jacob, his own life is spared, and, ultimately, through the successful encounter with his brother Esau that follows, his progeny, too, will be safe. In both cases, the change of name is accomplished through divine command.

Naomi's case stands in stark opposition to these examples. Instead of creating a covenant with God or wrestling with God's messenger, Naomi's experience is one of desertion and destruction by God. Naomi's family is forced to leave Bethlehem during a period of famine, which, from her perspective, God could well have prevented (or at least alleviated). Then God punishes her for leaving; as she says in verse 21, "I went full and the Eternal One has brought me back empty. Why do you call me Naomi? On the contrary the Eternal One answered me and Shaddai has dealt harshly with me."[30] God has wrought this terror on her, not someone else, and she certainly is not accepting personal responsibility for what has happened to her.

The use of Shaddai as a name of God is striking here. Shaddai occurs reliably forty-eight times in the Hebrew Bible, though thirty-one of those usages (i.e., nearly two-thirds of all the occurrences) are in the Book of Job. Why does Naomi choose this name to refer to God, both here and in verse 20, as the God who has embittered her and caused ill to befall her? No certain etymology for Shaddai has yet been derived, but that need not be the main concern here.[31] Instead, Naomi may be playing with the potential meanings of the appellation. Among the possible etymologies are "protective spirit" and "rescuer." Is Naomi pointing to the irony of a God who ought to be protecting her and rescuing her but instead causes harm and destruction? Another possible, though more likely reappropriated derivation is "breast."[32] Is Naomi calling out to God, who ought to be providing sustenance for failing to do so? Ernst Knauf notes that "not a single attestation [of Shaddai] refers to the level of 'family religion' . . . or links him [*sic*] specifically with Abraham or his clan."[33] Is Naomi subtly pointing out her distance from God in opposition to those other, more chosen figures whom God renames? After all, Naomi has to rename herself.

As the chapter draws to a close, in the final verse, Naomi is settled in Bethlehem with Ruth, who is referred to as both a Moabite and Naomi's daughter-in-law. This information should surely have been clear to all readers by now, yet the text repeats it. Naomi, who has declared herself broken and embittered in the previous two verses, is, in fact, *not* alone, though she is with someone who, by all social standards of the time, ought not to have mattered at all. And yet Ruth's demonstrable and outspoken commitment to Naomi will come to undermine these supposed norms. And the cliffhanger is that they have arrived at the beginning of the barley harvest.

NOTES

1. I recognize that these terms are anachronistic when applied to the Hebrew Bible, but they nevertheless describe a reality that would have been true then as well. A man, his woman, and children would then, too, have constituted the basic family unit. Of course, this basic family unit would have more normally resided within a larger family compound, made up of the husband's extended family. "In addition to the nuclear family of two parents and their unmarried children, the *bet 'ab* might include several generations of family members, as well as slaves, servants, and many others": Jennie R. Ebeling, *Women's Lives in Biblical Times* (London: T&T Clark, 2010), 27.

2. Naomi appears literally to mean "my kind one." For an explanation of the translation of "kindness of God" as the more likely meaning of the name, see Jeremy Schipper, *The Anchor Yale Bible: Ruth—A New Translation with Introduction and Commentary* (New Haven, CT: Yale University Press, 2016), 81.

3. Although the most-cited explanation for the use of the root .א.ש.נ ("lift up" in this context) is that it is Late Biblical Hebrew (i.e., Schipper, *The Anchor Yale Bible: Ruth*, 83), Gafney, "Mother Knows Best," 29, argues that the usage of this

root here should be understood as "rape-marriage," similar to its usage in Judg. 21:23.

4. One answer is Gafney's, that these were rape-marriages.

5. Ruth Rabbah 2:9. Eglon is the King of Moab (Judg. 3:13).

6. For an imaginative answer to those questions, see Athalya Brenner, *I Am . . . Biblical Women Tell Their Own Stories* (Minneapolis, MN: Fortress Press, 1985), 109.

7. Of course, the reconciliation of two women might equally refer to Ruth and Naomi, as I will discuss in the subsection "The Blessings (Ruth 4:11–12)" in chapter 12.

8. Mic. 7:6:

כִּי־בֵן֙ מְנַבֵּ֣ל אָ֔ב בַּ֚ת קָמָ֣ה בְאִמָּ֔הּ כַּלָּ֖ה בַּחֲמֹתָ֑הּ אֹיְבֵ֥י אִ֖ישׁ אַנְשֵׁ֥י בֵיתֽוֹ׃

For son spurns father, daughter rises up against mother, daughter-in-law against mother-in-law—a man's own household are his enemies.

An oblique reference to Rebekah's displeasure at Esau's Hittite wives is recorded in Gen. 26:34, though here both Rebekah *and* Isaac disapprove, and the text records nothing about either parent's relationship with their daughters-in-law. Clearly, the disapproval is enough to motivate Esau to take a wife from among his extended paternal family. In Gen. 28:8, however, only Isaac is mentioned in reference to this disapproval, where, after in Gen. 28:9, Esau takes Ishmael's daughter as a wife.

9. Marc Chagall, *Naomi, Ruth, and Orpah*, c. 1960, lithograph. Sometimes also referred to as *Naomi and Her Daughters-in-Law*.

For examples of using visual art for biblical commentary, see J. Cheryl Exum, *Art as Biblical Commentary: Visual Criticism from Hagar the Wife of Abraham to Mary the Mother of Jesus* (London: T&T Clark, 2019). Also see "The Visual Commentary on Scripture: Encounter the Bible through Art" at https://thevcs.org/, a project of the Theology and Religious Studies department, King's College London.

10. See, for example, Mieke Bal, *Lethal Love: Feminist Literary Readings of Biblical Love Stories* (Bloomington: Indiana University Press, 1987), 77, table 5. According to this table, Ruth and Naomi collectively speak twenty times. Boaz and *Peloni Almoni* speak fifteen times. The collective voices are evenly split between the women of Bethlehem and the elders at the gates.

11. For examples of derision, see Ruth Rabbah 2:9: "The name of the first was Orpah, because she turned her back on her mother-in-law." Also see *B. Sotah* 42b, where Orpah is associated with the mother of Goliath. Although 2 Sam. 21:16 identifies Goliath's mother as Harafah, Rav and Shmuel attempt to reconcile Harafah and Orpah as the same woman by playing on the meanings of their names in a highly sexualized fashion: "Her name is Harafah and why is she called Orpah? Because everyone came at her from behind [i.e., they sodomised her]."

For an example of championing Orpah, see Laura E. Donaldson, "The Sign of Orpah: Reading Ruth Through Native Eyes," in *A Feminist Companion to the Bible:*

Ruth and Esther (Second Series), edited by Athayla Brenner (Sheffield: Sheffield Academic Press, 1999), 130–144.

12. Cf. Donaldson, "The Sign of Orpah," 143: "To Cherokee women, for example, Orpah denotes hope rather than perversity, because she is the one who does not reject her tradition or her ancestors. Like Cherokee women have done for hundreds if not thousands of years, Orpah chooses the house of her clan and spiritual mother over the desires of another culture."

13. תיפלות can also mean frivolity or trivialness in Aramaic. The cognate Biblical Hebrew root can also mean impropriety or indecency. Jastrow, *Dictionary of the Targumim*, 1686–87.

14. Samuel's anointing of Saul.

15. Aaron greeting Moses when Moses returned from Midian with Zipporah.

16. קריבות (closeness) is from the same root as קרובתו (his relation).

17. ותשק ערפה לחמותה כל נשיקה של תיפלות בר מן תלת נשיקה של גדולה ונשיקה של פרקים ונשיקה של פרישות של גדולה דכתיב (שם י') ויקח שמואל את פך השמן ויצק על ראשו וישקהו של פרקים דכתיב (שמות ד') ויפגשהו בהר האלהים וישק לו של פרישות שנאמר ותשק ערפה לחמותה רבי תנחומא אמר אף נשיקה של קריבות שנאמר (בראשית כ"ט) וישק יעקב לרחל למה שהיתה קרובתו:

18. James Scott first describes the concept of hidden transcripts in his foundational work on the subject. See James C. Scott, *Domination and the Arts of Resistance: Hidden Transcripts* (New Haven, CT: Yale University Press, 1990). Scott describes how subordinated groups must express themselves in public to adhere to the expectations of those in power, the "public transcript." Sometimes, however, the subordinates break out and express themselves in what Scott terms a "hidden transcript." This concept has been little used in biblical studies, though a good example of its application can be found in Robert Williamson Jr., "Lament and the Arts of Resistance: Public and Hidden Transcripts in Lamentations 5," in *Lamentations in Ancient and Contemporary Cultural Contexts*, edited by Nancy Lee and Carleen Mandolfo (Atlanta: SBL, 2008), 67–80.

19. Schipper, *The Anchor Yale Bible: Ruth*, 97–98.

20. Schipper, *The Anchor Yale Bible: Ruth*, 98.

21. J. Cheryl Exum, *Plotted, Shot, and Painted: Cultural Representations of Biblical Women* (Sheffield: Sheffield Academic Press, 1996), 145. Also see note 36, 145–46, where Exum considers the Septuagint translation of דבקה as ηκολούθησεν (she followed after): "Could it be that the Septuagint translator sensed the erotic implications of translating *dbq* with a form of *kollaō* here and wanted therefore to avoid using the term? In a similar vein, the Septuagint translates ותשק (she kissed) earlier in the verse with the verb καταφιλεω, which appears to specifically refer to social, non-erotic kissing only, Muraoka, pg. 387."

22. Cf. Jon L. Berquist, "Role Differentiation in the Book of Ruth," *Journal for the Study of the Old Testament* 57 (1993): 26–27: "When Ruth clings to Naomi, Ruth takes the male role in initiating a relationship of formal commitment, similar to marriage."

Contra, Athayla Brenner, *The Intercourse of Knowledge: On Gendering Desire and "Sexuality" in the Hebrew Bible* (New York: Brill, 1997), 20:

Because the term [קבד ב] basically and tangibly has a primarily concrete physical reference ("be in very close proximity to"), it could have been expected that its signification within the "love" realm will be "sexual intercourse." This is certainly not so in the case of Ruth, who "loves" Naomi (Ruth 4.15) hence "clings to her" (1.14).

But Brenner never explains why it could not have been the case.

23. Schipper, *The Anchor Yale Bible: Ruth*, 98.

24. For example, the Cave of Machpelah, purchased by Abraham for Sarah's burial (Gen. 23) and in which all of the patriarchs and matriarchs (bar Rachel) were subsequently buried.

25. The protasis is implied in this statement but is, nevertheless, clear from the context. Cf. Donald R. Vance, *A Hebrew Reader for Ruth* (Peabody, MA: Hendrickson, 2003), 18–19; also Schipper, *The Anchor Yale Bible: Ruth*, 100.

26. "In love" need not denote a sexual desire for Naomi, but it is nevertheless a distinct possible reading.

27. Cross-dressing is, of course, expressly forbidden by Deut. 22:5:

לֹא־יִהְיֶה כְלִי־גֶבֶר עַל־אִשָּׁה וְלֹא־יִלְבַּשׁ גֶּבֶר שִׂמְלַת אִשָּׁה כִּי תוֹעֲבַת יְהוָה אֱלֹהֶיךָ כָּל־עֹשֵׂה אֵלֶּה:

A woman will not put on man's clothing and a man will not wear woman's clothing, because it is an abomination of the Eternal your God everyone who does these things.

But marrying a Moabite is forbidden by Deuteronomy (in the very next chapter), too. If the story can break one deuterocanonical law, why should it not break another? Indeed, the shock that the women of Bethlehem express might be even more comprehensible if they consider that Naomi is breaking religious law.

28. Gen. 17:1–15.

29. Gen. 32:25–33. See Gen. 49:2, where the names Jacob and Israel are used in parallel, for an example of Israel being used to refer to Jacob the man.

30. אֲנִי מְלֵאָה הָלַכְתִּי וְרֵיקָם הֱשִׁיבַנִי יְהוָה לָמָּה תִקְרֶאנָה לִי נָעֳמִי וַיהוָה עָנָה בִי וְשַׁדַּי הֵרַע לִי:

31. Georg Steins, "שדי/sadday," in *The Theological Dictionary of the Old Testament: Volume XIV*, edited by G. Johannes Botterweck and Helmer Ringgren (Grand Rapids, MI: William B. Eerdmans, 2004), 422: "Even after an examination of these various etymological explanations, one acknowledges that still no satisfactory etymology for *šadday* has been presented and that the resolution of its etymology will have to await the emergence of additional relevant materials." Cf. Ernst A. Knauf, "Shadday שדי," in *The Dictionary of Deities and Demons in the Bible*, edited by Karel van der Toorn, Bob Becking, and Pieter W. van der Horst (Leiden: E. J. Brill, 1995), 1416.

32. Knauf, "Shadday," 1419.

33. Knauf, "Shadday," 1419.

Chapter 3

Who Is Naomi?

וְשֵׁם הָאִישׁ אֱלִימֶלֶךְ וְשֵׁם אִשְׁתּוֹ נָעֳמִי

The name of the man was Elimelech, and his wife's name was Naomi.
(Ruth 1:2)

When the women of Bethlehem see Naomi on her return to the city, they cry out, "Is this Naomi?" (Ruth 1:20). As I have discussed previously, they know that the woman they are seeing simultaneously *is* Naomi and is somehow *not* Naomi. Something has changed in Naomi, though the women never overtly articulate what that might be.[1]

What sort of woman is Naomi? It is easy to slip into the presumption that all women are alike in their gender presentation, particularly when the woman in question is known to have married a man and birthed children. Yet, self-evidently, not all women are exactly the same, physically, psychologically, or emotionally. The way in which women present their gender identities is infinitely varied but too easily overlooked, particularly in the assumed heteropatriarchal world of the Hebrew Bible.[2]

In *Plotted, Shot, and Painted*, J. Cheryl Exum problematizes the question of Naomi's gender presentation through the examination of Philip Hermogenes Calderon's late nineteenth-century painting *Ruth and Naomi* (figure 3.1).[3]

Using the painting but without disclosing the title, she asks a wide range of people to identify the figures in the painting. Approximately half the people she asks identify the figure in black as Naomi, but just about as many identify this figure as Boaz.[4] Exum queries the apparently more masculine features of the figure in black, whom Calderon clearly intends to be Naomi. This Naomi is depicted as taller than Ruth; the dark clothing and headdress are distinctively different from those of the other two figures; even the facial features

Figure 3.1   Ruth and Naomi. *Source*: Philip Hermogenes Calderon, 1833–1898.

appear less soft. And, of course, Ruth gazes up into Naomi's face in a sort of rapturous, passionate fashion.[5] "Is this Naomi?"—a tall woman, holding a younger woman, gazing down into her desirous face?

Exum employs Calderon's painting and the ambiguity that it embodies as a means of discussing both heterosexual and homosexual readings of the love stories in Ruth (Ruth-Boaz and Ruth-Naomi). After a thorough examination of each, in a section titled "The Ruth-Naomi-Boaz Triangle," Exum writes,

> I want to suggest that the figure of Naomi in the Bible is as sexually ambivalent as the figure in black in Calderon's painting and that this ambivalence, in both the metatext and its source text, challenges our notions of gender by destabilizing our gender categories. . . . There is a striking blurring of gender roles, indeed of sexually determined roles—husband, wife, mother, father—in this tale, with Naomi symbolically holding all of four of these roles.[6]

Exum's more-than-quarter-of-a-century-old assertion is striking. She suggests that Naomi presents as "sexually ambivalent." Today, a panoply of different terms exists that might cover Naomi's possible gender presentations.

Figure 3.2   Ruth and Naomi. *Source*: Ary Scheffer, c. 1856.

What is important about Exum's insight is that it destabilizes the presumption that Naomi must be a cisgender, heterosexual woman.

Comparing Calderon's painting to the paintings of Naomi and Ruth presented subsequently, both also dating from the second half of the nineteenth century, can serve to further problematize the issue of Naomi's gender presentation (see figures 3.2 and 3.3).

Ary Scheffer's Naomi appears worn, with dark circles bagging under her eyes. She is solid, superficially seeming to be the same height as Ruth, but Ruth's head is clocked to the side, so perhaps Naomi is actually slightly shorter, possibly stockier, than Ruth. Naomi is neither especially young nor especially old. She is more tanned than Ruth, and her hands are larger and less smooth than Ruth's. Naomi is covered in great swathes of drapery, but it is neither alluring nor revealing. Only the thick cloth belt holding her clothes together reveals anything of a possible waistline. Her breasts are hidden from view by the placement of her arm. Though the attire denotes that Naomi is a woman, she is not an object of desire, nor does she appear to be desirous of Ruth. Unlike Ruth, who stares intently at Naomi, Naomi's gaze is just over

Figure 3.3 **Naomi and Ruth.** *Source*: Evelyn de Morgan, 1887.

Ruth's shoulder into the mid-distance. The road back to Bethlehem, perhaps the hard slog of the journey and the dangers it presents, or simply the ignominy of returning without a husband or sons, seems to be what Naomi is focused on, not sexual desire or even mere affection for the young women she is directing home by way of the outstretched arm with a finger pointed toward Orpah. This version of Naomi seems pragmatic and practical, a middle-aged woman in charge, almost as if she were acting functionally as a stereotypical man.

By way of contrast, Evelyn de Morgan's Naomi is tall, towering over Ruth, on whom she looks down. With one hand pulling Ruth's lush red hair over to the side, Naomi exposes the erogenous zone of the back of Ruth's neck. Their eyes are locked together. This Naomi is completely engaged with Ruth; their connection has a frisson about it. Unlike in Calderon's painting, in which only a small sliver of Naomi's face is visible, de Morgan paints Naomi as almost fully frontal so the viewer can see the majority of her face.[7] Her facial skin is as smooth as Ruth's. Her hair is covered, but her breastbone is exposed. The arm that is not behind Ruth's hair is outstretched, with Ruth's hand resting comfortably inside it. Ruth's other hand is on Naomi's shoulder. The women are locked together. Unlike in the other paintings, Orpah is nowhere to be seen. If Scheffer's Naomi is almost masculine and Calderon's Naomi is sexually ambivalent, de Morgan's Naomi is erotically charged, with Naomi clearly focused on Ruth and the emotion flowing between them.

These paintings problematize well the questions of Naomi's gender identity and sexual orientation. If Naomi might be something other than a cisgender, heterosexual woman, what textual clues are there about her gender presentation?

Naomi has lived a hard life, suffering famine and death in her immediate family. She also endured pregnancy and childbirth at least twice, both of which, until modern times, entailed substantial risks for women. She has interpersonal relationships with both women and men and inspires fierce loyalty in her daughters-in-law as well as the women of Bethlehem, who remember her after many years away, bless her, and assert her right to Ruth and Boaz's son as her own. She is capable of traveling long distances, not only with male support but also, and more important, on her own. She is assertive, taking the decision without consultation to return to Bethlehem and instructing her daughters-in-law to leave her. She instructs Ruth on how to arrange marriage to Boaz, displaying not only experience and daring but also strategic thinking (Ruth 3:1–4). She is able to formulate plans and see them through. Naomi has a strong voice that she uses to speak clearly when she wants to, while she is equally able to remain silent when she wants to. She is even capable of critiquing God and does so forcefully as culpable for her hardships.

What, if anything, does all of this hint at regarding Naomi's gender presentation? She comes across as a strong woman, both strong physically and strong willed. I am conscious of the problems of falling into the trap of gender essentialism; nevertheless, in not asking questions about Naomi's gender presentation and doing our best to excavate what we can from the text, we can equally fall into the trap of simply assuming that Naomi is a cisgender, heterosexual female (apparently the assumed position for women across the whole of the Hebrew Bible). So although these characteristics cannot tell us anything definitive about Naomi's gender presentation, what we can observe is that these characteristics are often, and especially in the heteropatriarchal society of the Hebrew Bible, most prominently associated with masculinity. I want to suggest, therefore, that a case exists for imagining Naomi as a masculinized woman.

In *Female Masculinities*, Jack Halberstam's foundational work, he traces the history of female masculinity from the eighteenth century onward before focusing on its various manifestations—tomboys, butch lesbians, drag kings, and dykes, for example—in more modern society. Halberstam is primarily concerned with female masculinities as they apply to same-sex sexuality, though he notes that "there is probably a lively history of the masculine heterosexual woman to be told, a history, moreover that must be buried by the bundling of all female masculinities into lesbian identity."[8] Female masculinity, thus, does not define sexual orientation. Crucially, therefore, in asking whether Naomi presents as a masculine woman, we should not assume that if she did, it would automatically make her either heterosexual or homosexual (or any other sexuality). Indeed, sexual orientation is not constrained by gender presentation.

If Naomi can be understood as a masculine woman about whose sexual orientation we should make no assumptions, should we also consider her gender presentation in terms of being transgender?[9] Jen Manion, writing about the eighteenth- and nineteenth-century phenomenon of female husbands in the United Kingdom and United States, uses "the concept of 'trans' as a verb," viewing the subjects of her book

> as traveling through life, establishing an ongoing and ever-unfolding relationship with gender, rather than viewing them as simply shifting between two unchanging binaries. Examining lives unfolding over time, we can consider how circumstance, age, and prior experiences with gender influenced their present and future decisions—as well as how others perceived these changes.[10]

Does Naomi go trans, presenting herself as more masculine, when it suits the situation in which she finds herself? Going back to Exum's observation that Naomi at times presents as "husband, wife, mother, father," does this not neatly fit Manion's description of "circumstance, age, and prior experiences"? Naomi can be the wife of Elimelech and mother of Mahlon and Chilion at the beginning of the story and then trans into the wife of Ruth and Orpah. Throughout the story, at times Naomi will present herself as fulfilling roles typical to either male or female biblical stereotypes. In viewing Naomi as "transing" when appropriate to the role she is inhabiting, we can see more clearly that Naomi does not need to adhere to "two unchanging binaries."

Within the context of a polyamorous family, Naomi would have had the ability to shift between the gender identities she wishes to express from the safety of what would appear to the rest of the world as a normative patriarchal family unit. She could more comfortably inhabit the space of a masculine woman who could trans depending on her interactions with different members of the family unit. A polyamorous family would be the perfect place for Naomi to be "husband, wife, mother, father," and much more besides.

NOTES

1. See chapter 2, subsection "From Triads to Dyads (Ruth 1:14–22)."

2. For example, see Deryn Guest's use of the concept of "genderfuck" to examine the ways in which Jael moves from seductress to "phallic murderer." Deryn Guest, "From Gender Reversal to Genderfuck: Reading Jael through a Lesbian Lens," in *Bible Trouble: Queer Reading at the Boundaries of Biblical Scholarship*, edited by Teresa J. Hornsby and Ken Stone (Atlanta: SBL Press, 2011), 9–44.

3. Exum, *Plotted, Shot, and Painted*, 129–37.

4. Exum, *Plotted, Shot, and Painted*, 130.

5. Exum, *Plotted, Shot, and Painted*, 130.

6. Exum, *Plotted, Shot, and Painted*, 169.

7. Naomi's face does tilt slightly at an angle, but her full face is not obscured.

8. Jack Halberstam, *Female Masculinities* (Durham, NC: Duke University Press, 1998), 57.

9. Cf. Guest, "Troubling the Waters," 51:

Transgender has often been used as an umbrella term into which a range of people can fit. A Finne Enke (2012, 4) thus notes how transgender might include "FTM, MTF, gender queer, trans woman, trans man, butch queen, fem queen, tranny, transy, drag king, bi-gender, pan-gender, femme, butch, stud, two spirit, people with intersex conditions, androgynous, gender-fluid, gender euphoric, third gender, *and* man and woman." Definitions in other sources inevitably add or omit terms, but the general sense of *transgender* as incorporating an assortment of lived experiences is clear.

10. Jen Manion, *Female Husbands: A Trans History* (Cambridge: Cambridge University Press, 2020), 11.

Chapter 4

Who Is Ruth?

וַיִּשְׂאוּ לָהֶם נָשִׁים מֹאֲבִיּוֹת שֵׁם הָאַחַת עָרְפָּה וְשֵׁם הַשֵּׁנִית רוּת

They lifted up for themselves Moabite wives, the name of one Orpah and the name of the second Ruth. (Ruth 1:4)

Ruth is a curious figure. On the one hand, she appears to be at the center of the book, the character on whom the entire story hangs. She is, after all, the eponymous protagonist of the book. Yet in reality, we know very little about her.

Ruth is a Moabite. The text refers to her as such on seven separate occasions (Ruth 1:4, 22; 2:2, 6, 21; 4:5, 10). But the text says nothing about her background—neither about her parents or any other genealogical information nor about her childhood or upbringing. She does not exist until she marries Mahlon, simply appearing in the text as having been taken in marriage by one of Naomi's sons. What we know about Ruth, we learn from her actions and her words as her story unfolds.

Even Ruth's name is not straightforward. Unlike virtually all of the other characters in the story, whose names have clear meanings that shed light on their characters, the root of the name Ruth is not clear. Various proposals have been put forward for the derivation of the name. Some commentators have associated רוּת (Ruth) with the word רְעוּת (Rʿût), meaning a female companion.[1] As Schipper points out, however, there is no compelling reason for the ע to have dropped out.[2] More recently, some commentators have tried to derive the name from a Moabite root, ryt, which appears in the Mesha Inscription and means "satiation."[3] Schipper finds this derivation equally dubious.[4] He similarly discounts other suggestions and suggests the most

53

likely derivation to be from the root .ה.ו.ר (*Rwh*), meaning "to be saturated with, drink one's fill of."[5] But the meaning is certainly far from clear.

Whether the meaning would have been clear to the ancient reader is a moot point. For the contemporary reader, it is perhaps part of the point that it will not be clear from the outset who Ruth is, whether encountering her in the title of the book or on her first appearance in Ruth 1:4. We come to Ruth, on a first reading at least, with little idea of what to expect from her: precisely because her name is not infused with meaning or even a clue. Additionally, no intertextual reference point in the Hebrew Bible exists for her based on her name. The modern reader can have no expectations of her until she begins to speak and act.

In that respect, until her now famous monologue in Ruth 1:16–17, Ruth is no different from Orpah, but with these words, Ruth transforms herself. In fact, speech is most often what transforms Ruth throughout the book. Although her actions are portrayed sympathetically—she goes out into the fields to glean and goes down to the threshing room floor (in accord with Naomi's instructions)—her use of language is really what marks her out. On more than one occasion, when she relays others' words, she does not repeat word for word what Naomi or Boaz have said but subtly transforms their utterances to create better outcomes for everyone.

Although much of the focus on Ruth's speech is on her declaration of commitment to Naomi in Chapter 1, it needs to be seen also in conjunction with her brief dialogs with Boaz in Chapters 2 and 3 and, importantly, with how Ruth relays information back to Naomi in both of these chapters. In Ruth 2:21, Ruth alters the instructions that Boaz has given her, though his words were never intended for Naomi's ears. In Ruth 3:17, Ruth doesn't so much alter as completely invent the words that Boaz has supposedly uttered regarding Naomi. In both of these situations, Ruth appears to be telling Naomi things that she believes will be best for Naomi to hear under the specific circumstances.

Additionally, in Ruth 3:9, Ruth embellishes Naomi's instructions for the threshing room floor scene. Naomi never tells Ruth what to say at all, only to wait for Boaz to tell her what to do. But in dialog with Boaz, Ruth uses her own initiative and her astute understanding of human nature to help Boaz appreciate the full weight of the situation between them.[6] Ruth is the one who mentions redemption to Boaz, utilizing the information relayed to her by Naomi (Ruth 2:20). As with Naomi, Ruth now tells Boaz the things that he most needs to hear.

As Naomi and Boaz are never described as having a direct dialog or otherwise interacting with each other at all, Ruth is the one mediating between them in the ways in which she speaks to each of them separately. Without Ruth, Boaz and Naomi apparently never communicated at all. Through

Ruth's subtle interventions, however, Naomi is made to feel that Boaz cares for her well-being (Ruth 3:17).[7] Although Boaz does not realize that Ruth's actions on the threshing room floor have anything to do with Naomi, nevertheless she is carrying out Naomi's instructions, which will have positive consequences for Boaz as well.

Ruth's ability to embellish, to say more than parsimony has required—indeed, in Ruth 1:16–17, she does so as well (she might more simply have said, "I swear to go wherever you go," and stop there)—sets her apart. Her words overflow with meaning. Although we might not have known from the outset what her name means, perhaps that is because we must first come to know her through the story and be saturated with her words before we can fully appreciate who she is. Ruth is the one whose words are filled with meaning and from whose mouth Naomi and Boaz must drink their fill. Ruth is the one drenched with enough emotional intelligence to fill them both.

NOTES

1. Cf. Esther 1:19.

2. Schipper, *The Anchor Yale Bible: Ruth*, 84.

3. Tamara Cohn Eskenazi and Tikva Frymer-Kensky, *The JPS Bible Commentary: Ruth* (Philadelphia: JPS, 2011), 6.

4. Schipper, *The Anchor Yale Bible: Ruth*, 84.

5. *DCH Vol VII* צ-ר, 426–27; Schipper, *The Anchor Yale Bible: Ruth*, 84.

6. For more details, see the subsection "Springing the Trap: The Encounter in the Night (Ruth 3: 6–15a)" in chapter 8 of this book.

7. Although Ruth also brings Naomi food in Ruth 2:18, neither the narrator nor the text describes this food as a gift from Boaz directly, but rather as Ruth's leftovers.

Chapter 5

Ruth 2

Building Relationships

INTRODUCING A MAN INTO THE PICTURE (RUTH 2:1–3)

Chapter 2 of the Book of Ruth opens with yet another familial relationship. In an inversion of the standard heteropatriarchal family introductions (such as the one in Ruth 1:1), Ruth 2:1 opens with Naomi. Rather than a man, his wife, and two sons, here we are presented with וּלְנׇעֳמִי (*ûləno ʿŏmî*), "and to Naomi," as the opening word and introduction to both the verse and the chapter. Although the reader is being introduced to Boaz, the text frames him in relation to Naomi, making her the crucial point of reference. Just at the point at which the reader may be concerned that Naomi has been left completely devoid of male kinship, the text presents a man to whom Naomi is somehow related via her deceased husband (though *how* is never clearly revealed). Although the story that is burgeoning will ostensibly be about the developing relationship between Ruth and Boaz, the entire premise hangs on their connections to Naomi.

Boaz is a "mighty man of valor," a man of means who is conveniently dropped into the plotline with no forewarning. And just as soon as he is inserted into the story, Ruth 2:2 moves the action on with Ruth requesting permission from Naomi to go gleaning in the fields. Ruth begins with the words אֵלֲכָה־נָּא (*ʾēləkāh-nā*), "please may I go," which are formed by the cohortative plus the particle נא. This formulation can be used "[t]o express a wish, or a request for permission, that one should be allowed to do something."[1] So although Ruth is speaking, again Naomi is the figure being centered here. Ruth consciously seeks and will not act without Naomi's prior approval.

Importantly, Ruth is not merely seeking approval to go glean in someone's fields to obtain food for them; she is specifically asking to אֶמְצָא־חֵן בְּעֵינָיו (*'emṣā'-ḥēn bə'ênāyw*), "find favor in his eyes." In other words, she is explicitly setting out to find the goodwill of someone else, someone other than Naomi, and, as is clear from the personal pronominal suffix, someone male. The language of finding favor is fairly commonplace in the Hebrew Bible, but spoken in the first person imperfect in direct dialog, it is less commonly used. Including the two usages in Ruth (here and in verse 13), this formulation occurs only seven times.[2] The phrase is far more commonly found in the first person perfect, almost entirely with the conditional particle אִם (*'m*; "if"), preceding it: אִם מָצָאתִי חֵן (*'m māṣā'ṯ ḥēn*), "if I have found favor [most commonly] in your [either singular or plural] eyes."[3] But the statement here made by Ruth is not attempting to leverage favor already found; rather, she is seeking Naomi's approval to go out and curry (as yet unfound) favor in the eyes of a male other.

The remaining occasions when the exact phrase *'emṣā'-ḥēn bə'ênāyw* occurs are as follows:

• Gen. 33:15, Jacob speaking to Esau
• Gen. 34:11, Shechem speaking to Jacob and his sons
• Exod. 33:13, Moses speaking to God
• 2 Sam. 15:25, David speaking to Zadok
• 2 Sam. 16:4, the servant of Mephibosheth speaking to David

On each of these occasions, the phrase is spoken by a male figure who might otherwise have been expected to be powerful to a male figure who has power over him.

In Gen. 33, Jacob repeatedly uses variations of this phrase when talking to Esau, his elder twin, whom he has not seen since manipulating him out of his birthright and blessing. Jacob is frightened of what Esau's reaction toward him will be. Even after Esau greets him as a brother, Jacob remains wary, constantly trying to curry favor. Finally, in verse 15, Esau offers to lend some of his men to accompany Jacob and his family as they travel onward, but Jacob refuses, saying, לָמָּה זֶּה אֶמְצָא־חֵן בְּעֵינֵי אֲדֹנִי (*Lāmmāh zeh 'emṣā'-ḥēn bə'ênê 'ăḏōnî*), "why this, my lord, I have found favor in your eyes." Jacob is being obsequious, for he remains unsure of his brother, who continues (at least in Jacob's estimation) to present a potential threat to his family. Conversely, in Gen. 34:11, Jacob and his sons are the powerful ones to whom Shechem, the son of the local Hivite chieftain, says *'emṣā'-ḥēn bə'ênāyw*. Shechem, used to the power of his position, is less accustomed to groveling, but, having already "defiled" Jacob's daughter Dinah, he knows he must show deference and thus uses this phrase.

In Exod. 33, Moses repeatedly uses the language of finding favor as he speaks with God. The Israelites have been caught out with the incident of the Golden Calf and punished severely. Moses knows he must negotiate the relationship between God and the people anew. The language of finding favor is key. In Exod. 33:13, Moses asks that if he, Moses, has found favor with God and if he knows God's ways, and then continues with *ʾemṣāʾ-ḥēn bə ʿênāyw*. The apodosis to this protasis is that God should then consider the Israelites as God's people. These words are those of a courtier talking to a king, and Moses is balancing them carefully. Finding favor here is about averting the possibility of an existential threat posed by the deity.

The final two examples involve David: once as he speaks to Zadok the priest in 2 Sam. 15:25 and once when Ziba, the servant of Mephibosheth, speaks to David in 2 Sam. 16:4. In both of these instances, *ʾemṣāʾ-ḥēn bə ʿênāyw* is used as part of the language of politics and courtiers, delicately handling highly charged situations. The language of finding favor works to defuse a potential threat and allows the more powerful party to acquiesce without relinquishing their authority and power.

Why then does Ruth, the only woman in the biblical text to utter these words, feel the need to do so with Naomi? Does Naomi really hold that kind of power over Ruth? Here in verse 2, the text reminds us, before Ruth begins to speak, that she is a Moabitess, a fact that all readers will already know full well. Could the insecurity she may feel from being a proscribed foreign woman play a role in how she is addressing Naomi here? More curiously, Ruth is not really employing the phrase in the same fashion as are the men discussed previously. They are all, in one way or another, using the phrase to try to defuse a difficult situation. They are not asking anyone for permission to go curry favor elsewhere; they are seeking to curry favor with the person(s) to whom they are speaking.

Ruth is not appealing to any favor she may already have in Naomi's eyes. She is laying out a plan and acknowledging that it will involve more than just obtaining food. She is looking for a way to find support, which will involve seeking the favor of a man. The implication is that by asking for Naomi's approval, any support she may find will work for the good of both of them. But below the surface of Ruth's request is also the prospect that Naomi may not respond well to the idea that Ruth needs to find favor in someone else's estimation—moreover, a man's estimation. If Ruth and Naomi already have an existing and closely bonded relationship, might Naomi be jealous of bringing someone else into it? Might the key here be that Ruth is concerned about how Naomi will react to the notion of Ruth needing to seek out the favor of a man?

But Naomi simply acquiesces, saying, "Go, my daughter." Is Naomi agreeing to Ruth seeking out someone else, or is she listening carefully to what is *not* said as much as to what *is* said? Can we hear Naomi assenting to Ruth seeking out someone *in addition to* them both? Perhaps, having had to acquiesce to marriage herself earlier in her life, when she was a younger woman capable of bearing children, Naomi understands that regardless of the feelings between Ruth and her, living within the limitations and confines of biblical society dictates that Ruth has no choice but to find male favor. And, just as Naomi has been able to cope with the strictures of heteropatriarchal marriage in the past, she is now once again resigned to that fate for her daughter-in-law and, conceivably, herself as well. And yet, the possibility of a polygamous marriage would easily allow for Naomi and Ruth to remain together under the shelter of an accommodating male. Maybe this knowledge-based thinking also informed Naomi's response.

With Naomi's consent, then, verse 3 states that Ruth goes off to glean in the fields, but really she is also going off to find favor in the eyes of some man. Perhaps the most surprising part of verse 3 is neither that she finds a field to reap in nor that said field belongs to Boaz, but rather that the text would have us believe that this situation is pure luck. Having already set up Boaz as Naomi's relative and as the "good guy" in verse 1, where else would the reader think Ruth was going to end up?

ENTER BOAZ (RUTH 2:4–16)

Verses 4–7 are largely a conversation between Boaz and the head of the men who reap in his fields. These verses depict Boaz arriving, noticing the new young woman reaping in his fields, and asking for more information. But the question is how we, as readers, understand his motivations. Commonly, this part of the story is interpreted as the beginning of the Boaz-Ruth romance. The tall, handsome, wealthy male landowner descends to his fields, only to be dazzled by a young, beautiful, single, sexually alluring, unknown, and mysterious foreign woman in need of rescue. The head of the reapers is just a transit device for conveying more information. But this interpretation is entirely dependent on a heteronormative reading of the situation.

Conversely, a homonormative reading may turn these assumptions on their heads.[4] Might Boaz actually be concerned about the effect this young woman might be having on the male reapers with whom he normally keeps company instead?[5] Boaz's instructions to Ruth in verse 8 might be understood as his concern for her safety, but, equally, instructing her to keep close to his young women could be an instruction to stay away from *his* young men, reinforced by the not-even-veiled threat of male violence in verse 9, if, essentially, she does not keep to her place. Boaz has the power to keep the male reapers from assaulting her, but this order is tied to her staying with the women. Yet if Ruth is already tied to Naomi in a homosexual relationship, then staying with the other women is actually more dangerous to her primary relationship. And if the whole point is to find favor in the eyes of a male protector, for both her own and Naomi's sake, then staying with the other women is not only potentially problematic for her relationship with Naomi but also at cross-purposes with one of her stated aims toward Naomi.

Hence, we should not be surprised to hear Ruth leap at Boaz's words as an assumption that מָצָאתִי חֵן בְּעֵינֶיךָ (*māṣā'tî ḥēn bə'ênêkā*), "I have found favor in your eyes." She is dissembling. Whatever his words might have meant, Ruth is putting a spin on them that she wants to make real. She has come to gain favor in the eyes of a man, and she has assumed, in innocence or not, that Boaz's words imply precisely this favor. He is now backed into a corner. Whether the hetero- or homo-normative reading applies to verses 4–7, he now must either contradict her assumptive reading of favor or play along with it.

His reply is deft. He does not capitulate to the binary choice between hetero- and homonormative readings of his motives. Instead, in verses 11–12, he takes the information that the head of his reapers has given him—that Ruth is the woman who returned from Moab with Naomi—and spins it out. Clearly, Boaz is a man who knows the town gossip, because in his explanation of why he is being kind to Ruth, he expounds all of the good things that Ruth has done since Mahlon's death. Boaz knows far more about Ruth than the mere fact that she is the woman who returned from Moab with Naomi. Boaz treats her well, not because of any sexual desires on his part (or certainly not any that he overtly expresses) but because Ruth has behaved beyond the bounds of what was necessary respecting her mother-in-law, Naomi. Again, Naomi is built into the fabric of the Ruth-Boaz relationship.

Ruth's reply in verse 13 demonstrates her proficiency in showing just the right amount of deference. Here, she presumes nothing about Boaz's motives. Rather, she treats the conversation as any courtier would, speaking to Boaz in a submissive fashion. She uses *'emṣā'-ḥēn bə'ênāyw*, as she did already with Naomi in verse 2, demonstrating precisely the implication of the phrase, as I have discussed previously. She then ends with the acknowledgment that she is not even as important to him as one of his female servants.

Both Ruth and Boaz know exactly what they are doing in speaking to each other this way. They are not enacting a love story.[6] They are crafting the highly specialized language of deference and power. Boaz may or may not be interested in a longer game. Ruth certainly is. And bridging the otherwise too great distance between them lies the connection: Naomi.

As their conversation concludes, Boaz invites Ruth to sit down and eat. She finds her place among the other reapers. But this gesture of partaking of food with his household is a significant act of hospitality. He hands her food as well, and she eats—not just a small amount, but her fill—until she is sated.

She even has leftovers. Again, this short scene in verse 14 is telling. For a woman who otherwise has no power or status to eat in this way in the home of a powerful man of stature whom she has only just met demonstrates much self-confidence on her part. Ruth's words may be full of deference, but she is poised enough to eat until she is full and still have some left over.

When the meal concludes, in verses 15–16, Boaz instructs his male reapers not only to allow Ruth to reap without interference but also to pull out extra stalks and leave them for her to glean. What are his motivations here? Clearly, he is protecting and providing for her, albeit in a fashion that allows her to feel that she is providing for herself. But his words leave a lacuna in the text because they lend no explanation as to *why* he does these things. Again, as readers, we must probe our own assumptions about the story we are reading. A heteronormative reading can easily view Boaz as acting out of romantic desire for Ruth. A homonormative reading might see Boaz as courting or overcompensating, being more kind than necessary, lest anyone think that he doesn't desire Ruth. Or perhaps he is simply trying to ensure that his reputation is preserved. A widow on his estate being molested and then starving to death with her mother-in-law, who is his kin, would not reflect well on him. Another option is that he could genuinely be a decent, God-fearing human being who understands his duty under Jewish law to ensure that the vulnerable, widowed woman reaping on his estate is protected and fed. For all we know, Boaz may treat any vulnerable person on his estate this way. His reapers certainly do not express surprise at their instructions from Boaz.

RETURNING TO NAOMI (RUTH 2:17–23)

Ruth goes back out to the fields, reaping until the evening. When she returns to Naomi, she does so with both food—around an *ephah* of barley and her leftovers from the meal—and news of her day's encounter with Boaz. Only now do we realize that, at least in Naomi's estimation, what has happened is exceptional. Naomi is surprised by the generosity paid to Ruth. To what extent does Naomi know what Ruth should have expected, reaping in the fields? Naomi has been away for more than ten years. The people of Bethlehem have lived through a period of famine. Things may have changed as the circumstances of the town and its inhabitants changed during Naomi's absence. We also know that Naomi is especially bitter (cf. Ruth 1:20–21). Might those experiences and her ensuing mental state have made her particularly prone to assuming the worst would continue to befall her and Ruth?

In that context, Naomi's enthusiastic response to Ruth's story makes more sense. Even before Ruth reveals Boaz's name to Naomi, Naomi blesses the man who has shown such generosity to Ruth. When Naomi finally does hear that the man in question is Boaz, something else comes into play in her response. She uses the word חסד (*hesed*) to describe the situation.[7] And only now does she see fit to mention that Boaz is מִגֹּאֲלֵנוּ (*Miggō ʾălēnû*), our redeemer. Why didn't she tell Ruth that in the first place? Wouldn't it have been sensible to advise Ruth to glean there from the outset? Had Naomi forgotten about Boaz? Did Naomi not think Boaz would have been kind and generous to Ruth? Was some part of Naomi jealous and disgruntled that Ruth was deliberately setting out to find male favor, so she deliberately overlooked the man who was best placed to provide it? Or did she think that Boaz didn't swing that way and would not be likely to warm to Ruth's charms?

Moreover, Naomi's speech here may provide a hidden transcript that breaks through. She refers to Boaz as "close to *us*"/"a relation of *ours*" and "*our* redeemer." Where the former is simply a statement of fact—Boaz is related to Naomi through her deceased husband and, by extension, also related to Ruth—she also refers to Boaz as a redeemer *for both of them*. At no other point in the narrative up to now has Naomi suggested that she, too, might be redeemed. A mere four verses later, at the beginning of Chapter 3, Naomi will suggest that she needs to find a solution for Ruth's situation. But here is a hint that she sees herself in that solution as well. Boaz is neither her (Naomi's) redeemer nor only Ruth's redeemer; he is *their* redeemer. In this slip of the tongue, where she might simply have said something like "Boaz is our relation and can also, therefore, be your redeemer," her hidden transcript breaks out. She could easily be implying that Naomi and Ruth are a package deal and require joint redemption.

Ruth, however, does not reply to the implications of Naomi's speech. Instead, she matches what she reads as Naomi's enthusiasm with her own further exposition. Verses 21–22 contain yet another peculiar exchange. Ruth tells Naomi that Boaz has instructed her עִם־הַנְּעָרִים אֲשֶׁר־לִי תִּדְבָּקִין (*ʾim-hanna ʿārîm ʾăser-lî tidbāqîn*), "cling to the young men who are mine," though in verse 8 Boaz tells her explicitly תִדְבָּקִין עִם־נַעֲרֹתָי (*Tidbāqîn ʾim-na ʿărōṯāi*), to "cling with my young women." Why does Ruth relay this not-quite-truth to Naomi? Why doesn't she tell her that Boaz instructed her to cling to his young women? We have already seen that Ruth is astute and selective in her use of language; her switch here cannot be accidental.

The language of "clinging" is crucial. In Ruth 1:14, as discussed previously, the text uses precisely this verb, דָּבַק (*Dābaq*), to describe how Ruth clings to Naomi. The connotations, particularly within the context of Ruth's monologue (Ruth 1:16–17), make plain that when Ruth clings to someone, it is a profound act, deep and resonant with meaning, potentially signaling a homosexual commitment on Ruth's behalf. How can Ruth now "cling" to the women in Boaz's field if she is already thus committed to Naomi? In changing Boaz's instructions, she speaks from her relationship with Naomi, not the presumed heteropatriarchal norms, and assumes that Naomi will feel less threatened by Ruth clinging to young men than to young women. But Naomi knows that the homosocial world that she and Ruth have been inhabiting is not the world of Bethlehem. In order to fit in and not give rise to suspicion, Ruth will need to cling to the young women; hence, Naomi corrects Ruth in her response. Naomi knows that the young men may assault her but the young women will not. Naomi does care for Ruth's well-being and safety and can put aside her own potential jealousy to ensure it.

The chapter draws to a close with another of the book's ambiguous time lapses. Ruth, as per Naomi's instructions, continues to glean in Boaz's field alongside the other women until both the barley and wheat harvests are complete. At what point in the harvest season did Ruth join them? How much longer, therefore, did she continue to glean in Boaz's fields? Did she encounter Boaz again during this period? What was Naomi doing during this time? These questions are not irrelevant, and I will return to them later in my discussion of Chapter 4. Chapter 2 finally ends with Ruth remaining with her mother-in-law, though the action of the next chapter will pick up during the threshing season, so it cannot be too much later after the harvest is completed.

NOTES

1. Arthur Ernest Cowley and Emil Kautzsch, *Gesenius' Hebrew Grammar* (Oxford: Clarendon Press, 1910), 320.

2. Additionally, in Gen. 47:25, the phrase is spoken by the people to Joseph in the first person plural.

3. Cf. Berquist, "Role Differentiation in the Book of Ruth," 28 note 11.

4. Hugh Pyper, "Boaz Reawakened: Modelling Masculinity in the Book of Ruth," in *Interested Readers: Essays on the Hebrew Bible in Honor of David J. A. Clines*, edited by James K. Aitken, Jeremy M. S. Clines, and Christl M. Maier (Atlanta: SBL, 2013), 452.

5. For a more detailed discussion of this reading, see chapter 7 of this book, "Who Is Boaz?"

6. Though that does not preclude the possibility that they might not also be flirting.

7. See chapter 6, "חסד *Hesed*: An Excursus," for a fuller explanation of this term and its relevance to the story.

Chapter 6

חסד *Hesed*

An Excursus

"The Eternal One will do *hesed* with you." (Ruth 1:8) Rabbi Zeira says, "This Megillah does not have anything in it about impurity or purity or what is forbidden and what is permitted. So why was it written? To teach us how great is the reward for acts of *hesed.*"

—Ruth Rabbah 2:14[1]

The term *hesed* is famously used on three occasions in the Book of Ruth and, as evidenced by Rabbi Zeira's comment, is considered a key component to unlocking the story.[2] But what is *hesed,* and how does it function within the Book of Ruth? I will argue that not only is *hesed* a major theme of the story, but, more excitingly, interlocking usages of *hesed* between Ruth, Naomi, and Boaz also fundamentally underpin a polyamorous reading of the Book of Ruth.

The term *hesed* has no exact equivalent in English. In the Book of Ruth, it is variously translated depending on the context. So, for example, in Ruth 1:8 and 2:20, NJPS and NRSV render "kindness" or "deal kindly" for *hesed,* but in Ruth 3:30 both versions translate it as "loyalty." The *Dictionary of Classical Hebrew* defines *hesed* as "loyalty, faithfulness, kindness, love, mercy."[3] Whereas all of these terms may exist on a continuum of meaning for English speakers, they are not equivalent terms, nor is there a word that conveniently rolls all of these meanings into one.

Indeed, several treatises have been written on the meaning of the term *hesed* in the Hebrew Bible, beginning in 1926 with Norman Glueck.[4] The subsequent research has been well summarized first by Katharine Doob Sakenfeld in her 1978 book, *The Meaning of Hesed in the Hebrew Bible: A New Inquiry,* and later by Gordon R. Clark in 1993 in *The Word Hesed in the Hebrew Bible.*[5]

Sakenfeld separates her own study of *hesed* into the term's use by human beings and by God. She further differentiates between its usage in pre-exilic and post-exilic settings, as well as in prose, narrative, prophetic literature, and other texts (proverbs, psalms, and related literature). In the case of the Book of Ruth, rather than reading all three usages together as part of the Ruth narrative, she views them separately, under different headings, as part of her wider investigation into the meaning of the term.[6] Problematically, Sakenfeld includes the Book of Ruth as pre-exilic prose, a categorization that is by no means certain.[7] Ultimately, however, she suggests a broad definition for *hesed* as "deliverance or protection as a responsible keeping of faith with another with whom one is in a relationship," though she admits that this definition is "extremely cumbersome" and still "does not cover the full range of meaning."[8] In particular, regarding the pre-exilic usage of *hesed* in a human context, she notes that *hesed* is "never a special favour; rather it is always a provision for an essential need" and "normally provides deliverance from dire straits."[9] Sakenfeld also notes the power dynamic within *hesed* as

> an action performed for the weak party by the powerful one. . . . Because of his [*sic*] powerful status, the superior party is always free not to perform the act of *hesed*; the weak party will have no opportunity to "get even" and no outside recrimination or interference . . . is to be feared. Nevertheless, the potential actor has a privately and even publically recognised responsibility to do *hesed* because of the relationship in which he [*sic*] stands. . . . Furthermore, the superior party is normally the sole source of assistance available to the party in need; if the powerful one does not act, the need will be met with disaster. . . . The actor may or may not have a measure of self-interest in his [*sic*] action.[10]

This element of power dynamics in acts of *hesed* will be especially important to consider when looking at the dynamics among Ruth, Boaz, and Naomi, particularly in trying to determine whether a version of polyamorous polygamy is possible between the three of them or whether they are interminably bound to the rules of patriarchal polygamy of the Hebrew Bible.

Rather than looking at the word in isolation, Clark attempts to build a lexical field for the study of *hesed*, looking at six roots that deal with "attributes that are relevant to interpersonal relationships"—namely, אמן and ,שנא ,אהב ,רחם ,חנן ,חסד (*ḥsd, ḥnn, rḥm, 'hḇ, šn', and 'mn*).[11] Like Sakenfeld, Clark scatters his discussion of the three examples of *hesed* in the Book of Ruth with specific dates for Ruth. In the end, Clark defines *hesed* as

> not merely an attitude or an emotion; it is an emotion that leads to an activity beneficial to the recipient. The relative status of the participants is never a feature of the חֶסֶד act, which may be described as a benefit action performed, in the context of a deep and enduring commitment between two persons or parties, by

one who is able to render assistance to the needy party who in the circumstances is unable to help him- or herself.[12]

Additionally, Clark determines that *hesed* is predominantly a "characteristic of God rather than human beings" but that ultimately it is "a supreme human virtue, standing as the pinnacle of moral values."[13] Finally, in summarizing his findings from the lexical field of *hesed*, he writes that

1. שנא [hate] is far from חֶסֶד;
2. חֶסֶד is closely related to חנן; it includes "grace" and "mercy," but it is much more than grace and mercy;
3. חֶסֶד is close to רחמים; it includes "compassion," but it is not merely compassion;
4. חֶסֶד is close to אמונה; it includes "faithfulness," "reliability," "confidence," but it is not merely faithfulness, reliability, confidence;
5. חֶסֶד is not very close to אהב; while it includes "love," its connotations are much broader than those of love.[14]

Overall, his definition suggests a sort of recipe for *hesed*, which might be the best way to describe it—add equal parts grace and mercy; a healthy dose of compassion; a large measure each of faithfulness, reliability, and confidence; and a dash of love for flavor—no hatred required. In short, *hesed* contains all of the ingredients for long-lasting, stable interpersonal relationships.[15] Mercy, compassion, and reliability with only a dash of love may all sound rather pedestrian and pragmatic compared to notions of romantic love as developed in eighteenth- and nineteenth-century English romantic novels, but these qualities are in many ways a more solid foundation for sustainable relationships. Clark's recipe for *hesed*, with its wider-ranging qualities rather than merely contemporary notions of romantic love, will serve as the basis for how *hesed* and the blessings associated with it could underpin the reading of a polyamorous relationship among Naomi, Ruth, and Boaz.

Turning toward the use of *hesed* in the Book of Ruth requires a close examination of the three verses in which the term is used. *Hesed* appears in Ruth 1:8, 2:20, and 3:10, each of which is discussed in turn subsequently.

Ruth 1:8

וַתֹּאמֶר נָעֳמִי לִשְׁתֵּי כַלֹּתֶיהָ לֵכְנָה שֹּׁבְנָה אִשָּׁה לְבֵית אִמָּהּ (יעשה) [יַעַשׂ] יְהוָה עִמָּכֶם חֶסֶד כַּאֲשֶׁר עֲשִׂיתֶם עִם־הַמֵּתִים וְעִמָּדִי:

Naomi said to her two daughters-in-law, "Go, return to the house of her mother. The Eternal One will do *hesed* with you as you did with the dead and with me!"

Following the deaths of Mahlon and Chilion, Naomi hears that there is now food in Bethlehem and begins the journey back. Somewhere along the road to Bethlehem, she turns to her daughters-in-law, Ruth and Orpah, and tries to persuade them to go back to their mothers' houses rather than continue on the journey to Bethlehem with her. Naomi's opening plea in this conversation (Ruth 1:8) begins by enjoining Orpah and Ruth to go back. Naomi then exhorts the Eternal One to do *hesed* with her daughters-in-law, just as Ruth and Orpah have done *hesed* both with the dead and with her, Naomi.

One major issue with the verse is the קרי כתיב (*qere ketiv*) halfway through.[16] יַעֲשֶׂה (*ya'ăseh*), "he will do," the third-person masculine singular imperfect is written (*ketiv*), but יַעַשׂ (*ya'as*), "he may do" or "let him do," is the *qere*, a third-person masculine singular jussive. The difference in meaning is subtle but important. Reading the simple imperfect makes Naomi sound as though she is issuing a statement of fact. By contrast, the jussive in Biblical Hebrew is volitive in mood, expressing a desire, making Naomi's speech not a statement of fact but an act of calling on God's will, a prayer or wish fulfillment, or perhaps even a demand.

The reading of the jussive here is strengthened by the use of a jussive as Naomi continues speaking to Orpah and Ruth (v 9)—יִתֵּן יְהוָה לָכֶם (*yittēn 'ădōnāi lākem*), "May the Eternal One give you." Although Naomi uses a word of the root ע.שׂ.ה ('*sh*), "do," rather than ב.ר.כ (*brk*), "bless" (as in Ruth 2:20 and 3:10), the force of both appears to be much the same. Naomi is petitioning the Eternal One to do *hesed* to Ruth and Orpah, which is much like a blessing. Verse 9 qualifies in some sense what that *hesed* or blessing might be—finding each woman rest in the house of a husband.

In sum, Naomi petitions the Eternal One to do *hesed* to Orpah and Ruth, who themselves have displayed *hesed* to the dead and Naomi.

Ruth 2:20

וַתֹּאמֶר נָעֳמִי לְכַלָּתָהּ בָּרוּךְ הוּא לַיהֹוָה אֲשֶׁר לֹא־עָזַב חַסְדּוֹ אֶת־הַחַיִּים וְאֶת־הַמֵּתִים וַתֹּאמֶר לָהּ נָעֳמִי
קָרוֹב לָנוּ הָאִישׁ מִגֹּאֲלֵנוּ הוּא:

Naomi said to her daughter-in-law, "Blessed be he to the Eternal One who did not forsake his *hesed* to the living and to the dead." Naomi said to her, "The man is close to us; he is from our one who redeems."

Toward the end of Chapter 2, Ruth has returned to Naomi after reaping in Boaz's field. Bringing food home with her—both what she had reaped and the leftovers from her meal with Boaz and his reapers—Naomi has many questions for Ruth about where she has been and whom she has met who has taken such generous notice of her. Ruth replies that she has been reaping in Boaz's field. Ruth 2:20 is Naomi's response before Ruth tells Naomi anything more about her experience beyond identifying Boaz.

The well-established difficulty with this verse concerns the identification of the antecedent for the relative pronoun אֲשֶׁר (*ăšer*) and the subsequent third-person masculine pronominal suffix appended to *hesed*, חַסְדּוֹ (*hasdô*), which could refer equally well to יהוה (*Adonai*) as to Boaz. Commentators are fairly evenly divided on the subject. Yoo-ki Kim's paper "The Agent of Ḥesed in Naomi's Blessing (Ruth 2,20)" usefully summarizes the arguments from antiquity onward. The Septuagint, Vulgate, and Targum all retain the ambiguity of the original Biblical Hebrew.[17] Among the major modern translations, no consensus exists.[18] Among contemporary commentators, some are in favor of Boaz as the referent, some *Adonai*, and still others prefer to live with the ambiguity, though, as Kim asserts, there is no reason to believe that the author intended ambiguity here.[19]

Kim turns instead to three main areas of investigation, including both syntactic analysis and thematic questions. Kim identifies *ăšer*, the relative pronoun, as introducing a relative clause, though the antecedent remains unclear. Normally, the antecedent would be the closest suitable noun to the relative pronoun, which in this case would be *Adonai*; however, Kim suggests that on its own, this location is not sufficient grounds to identify *Adonai* as the antecedent. Indeed, Kim goes on to posit that either the original word order has been inverted (בָּרוּךְ לַיהוָה הוּא became the current text, בָּרוּךְ הוּא לַיהוָה) or the relative clause was too long for its more correct position (בָּרוּךְ הוּא אֲשֶׁר לֹא־עָזַב חַסְדּוֹ אֶת־הַחַיִּים וְאֶת־הַמֵּתִים לַיהוָה)—hence the confusion.[20] Additionally, Kim examines a number of structurally similar verses, eventually concluding that "[o]ur analysis favors Boaz as the agent of *hesed*."[21]

Kim turns his attention to the themes of "*hesed* for the living and the dead" and "the Book of Ruth and Naomi's blessing."[22] On both themes, Kim makes a strong case in favor of reading Boaz as the antecedent of the relative pronoun. Several of his points in these regards are worth reiterating here. God never performs *hesed* for the dead anywhere in the Hebrew Bible, a notion that would have been anathema to ancient Israelite religion.[23] Associating *hesed* to the dead with Boaz, rather than God, therefore makes far more sense. As for Naomi's blessing, God, though ever present in the background of the Book of Ruth, never intervenes directly in the story, making it unlikely that Naomi is blessing God's *hesed* rather than Boaz's.[24] Moreover, "[j]ust as Boaz's blessing of Ruth is followed by the grounds for it in R 3,10, the relative clause in Ruth 2,20 can best be interpreted as grounds for which Naomi blesses Boaz."[25]

Overall, Kim makes a strong case for the identification of Boaz as the antecedent of the relative pronoun and the subject of the relative clause. That Boaz is the one who performs *hesed* to the living and the dead seems a reasonable conclusion and one that will be important in understanding the relationship among Boaz, Ruth, and Naomi.

Accepting the aforementioned arguments in favor of Boaz as the subject of the relative clause, in summary, in this verse Naomi blesses Boaz, who has displayed *hesed* to Naomi's living (i.e., Ruth) and deceased relations.

Ruth 3:10

וַיֹּאמֶר בְּרוּכָה אַתְּ לַיהֹוָה בִּתִּי הֵיטַבְתְּ חַסְדֵּךְ הָאַחֲרוֹן מִן־הָרִאשׁוֹן לְבִלְתִּי־לֶכֶת אַחֲרֵי הַבַּחוּרִים אִם־דַּל וְאִם־עָשִׁיר:

He said, "Blessed are you to the Eternal One, my daughter. You have acted benevolently; the last of your *hesed* is greater than the first in not going after young men whether poor or rich."

This final usage of *hesed* in the Book of Ruth comes amid the scene on the threshing room floor between Ruth and Boaz. Ruth, having followed Naomi's instructions, goes down to the threshing room floor. She notes where Boaz, who has drunk and eaten until well satiated and cheerful (perhaps intoxicated), lies down, and there she lies down herself. Where exactly Ruth lies down is the subject of some speculation, but certainly it is somewhere near the lower half of Boaz's body. The text is equally ambiguous about whom she undresses and how much of the body is undressed, but certainly by the time Boaz is startled awake, at least one of them is only partially clothed. Boaz is unnerved by this situation as he wakes up, asking who is there. Ruth replies that it is she and that she has come to ask him to act as a redeemer.

Next, Boaz properly finds his voice (Ruth 3:10), beginning a complex response to Ruth that will last for four verses in total. He begins by blessing Ruth; his response, בְּרוּכָה אַתְּ לַיהֹוָה (*bərûkāh 'at la'dōnāi*), is phrased precisely like Naomi's earlier one to Ruth (Ruth 2:20), בָּרוּךְ הוּא לַיהֹוָה (*bārûk hû' la'dōnāi*). Although no relative pronoun or clause is employed here, as in Ruth 2:20, the sense of dependence is the same. He blesses Ruth because of her benevolence and *hesed*. He states that her current act of *hesed*, not pursuing younger men, is greater than her first act of *hesed*.[26] Her first act must implicitly refer to her conduct toward Naomi (table 6.1).[27]

In sum, Boaz blesses Ruth, who displays *hesed* to both Boaz and Naomi. Overall, in each of the uses of *hesed* in the Book of Ruth, we have identified persons offering a blessing or petition, persons displaying *hesed* through their actions, and persons to whom this *hesed* has been displayed. From table 6.1, we can see that Ruth never blesses/petitions, but she both displays and receives *hesed*.[28] Naomi never displays *hesed*, but she both petitions for *hesed* on behalf of others and receives *hesed*. Boaz, however, blesses, displays

Table 6.1 An Analysis of the Use of *Hesed* in the Book of Ruth

Verse	1:8	2:20	3:10
Who speaks in blessing/ petition	Naomi petitions (ya'aś Adonai) for hesed	Naomi blesses (Bārûk hû' la'dōnāi)	Boaz blesses (Bārûk hû' la'dōnāi)
Who displays *hesed*	Ruth and Orpah	Boaz	Ruth
Who is the recipient of *hesed*	Naomi and the dead	Ruth and the dead	Boaz (and Naomi)

hesed, and receives *hesed*. The Ruth-Naomi dyad is inherently unstable, as they are not entirely reciprocal with each other—Naomi is capable of petitioning for *hesed* for Ruth but not of displaying it herself. Ruth is capable of displaying *hesed* to Naomi, but she cannot petition on her behalf or bless her. Boaz, however, *can* bless Ruth and display *hesed* toward her and the dead (of Naomi's family), *and* Boaz is the recipient of *hesed* from Ruth and of blessing from Naomi.

Simplifying the matter further:

- Only Naomi and Boaz can bless.
- Only Ruth and Boaz can display *hesed*.
- Naomi, Ruth, and Boaz can all be recipients of *hesed*.

Why is Ruth incapable of blessing others? Why is Naomi incapable of displaying *hesed* to others? Why is Boaz capable of all three? The answers lie, perhaps, in each of their personal qualities, as well as in the power dynamics between them.

Naomi is damaged by the trauma of the deaths of her husband and sons and possibly too caught up in the challenges of trying to fit into her own skin to be able to give too much back to anyone. *Hesed* requires a surfeit, going beyond what is normally expected, which may be beyond Naomi's current capacities. Ruth the Moabitess knows how to behave toward other humans, but she has yet to settle enough into her relationship with God that she is able to call on God for the sake of others. But as the member of the trio who displays the most *hesed*, this abundance may also point back to the possible meaning of her name as "to be saturated with." Ruth is the one so saturated with *hesed* that it overflows from her. Finally, Boaz, while not married, is nevertheless a wealthy landowner and man of stature in Bethlehem. He has the capacity to give beyond what is required of him, and he evidently maintains a level of comfort in his own relationship with God. But until he meets Ruth and Naomi, he appears to have no one to give back to.

As to the power dynamic between the parties, Sakenfeld points to the importance of understanding relationships involving *hesed*. The question, then, is this: Who has power over whom in this triad? As an adult Israelite male landowner in a patriarchal society, Boaz is clearly near the top of the power pyramid of biblical Israel. As such, he can be assumed to hold more social capital than either Naomi or Ruth—hence, he has the ability to walk away from both Ruth and Naomi. He is not obligated to treat either of them with *hesed*. Perhaps this freedom to choose is precisely why Boaz is able both to bless and to perform *hesed* as well as receive *hesed*.

Naomi, conversely, is an Israelite widow who is no longer able to bear children. As a widow, Naomi is among the weakest members of the Israelite community and one who requires the protection of others. She has no power over anyone, save perhaps her daughters-in-law. But her daughters-in-law are foreigners, Moabites, who are ostensibly proscribed from marriage into the Israelite community, meaning that in a purely instrumental sense they are of little practical use to her. Of Boaz, Ruth, and Naomi, Naomi is the weakest, and although she might be seen to hold little social capital, clearly she is portrayed as having strong interpersonal relationships. Her daughters-in-law love her, with Ruth vowing to remain with Naomi despite Naomi's best attempts to persuade her otherwise. The women of Bethlehem also clearly have some residual social relationship with Naomi, remembering her and speaking to her despite an absence of more than ten years and some form of physical and/ or psychological change during that period. But Naomi has limited room to maneuver given the constraints of her place within Israelite society, which may explain why she feels able to call on God to provide blessings to others but has no space to offer any of her own. From her weaker position, she is also in a prime place to receive *hesed*.

Ruth's position is more challenging and less straightforward than that of either Boaz or Naomi. Ruth is young enough to be considered marriageable, but she is also a proscribed foreigner and the widow of an Israelite. Within the structure of Israelite society, she is anomalous. She ought simply to have gone back to her mother's house, as her sister-in-law Orpah did, but Ruth defies this straightforward option for categorization. What power could she have wielded in such a situation? As a foreigner whose alignment with Israelite society and religion is still being established, she remains weak and an easy recipient of *hesed*. What perhaps marks Ruth out as exceptional is that even from her weak position, she is able to offer *hesed* to others. She ought not to be able to, but she does so by breaking free of the power structures that normally dominate *hesed*. Her mother-in-law ought to have had some power over her, and yet Ruth is the one who behaves with *hesed*. Boaz certainly has far more power over her than she over him, and yet Boaz asserts that Ruth is the one who behaves toward *him* with *hesed*. Here Naomi has deftly judged that Ruth has some small amounts of power as a marriageable woman and directed Ruth to use that power to seduce Boaz into marriage. Yet Boaz still understands this action not as manipulation but as *hesed*. Ruth, the outsider, may not be able to bless, but she is able to disrupt the normal boundaries of power dynamics, using her weakness to receive *hesed* and her outsider status to offer *hesed*.

Crucially, as a triad, then, they complete each other like interconnected puzzle pieces. They each require one another.[29] And the first three chapters of the Book of Ruth knot them together in this complex bonding of blessing and *hesed*. As dyadic relationships, they would miss some element—blessing, receiving *hesed*, or performing *hesed*. As a triad, they balance each other out.

Of the four chapters in the Book of Ruth, only the first three chapters employ the term *hesed*, each doing so only once. But in the final chapter, the term is absent, a curiosity in and of itself. What is the reader to make of the absence of *hesed* in this final chapter? Is the purpose of *hesed* finished and thus no longer necessary to mention? Or perhaps, rather than an absence of *hesed*, Chapter 4 is simply the living embodiment or demonstration of an abundance of *hesed*. If so, then in what ways do Ruth, Naomi, and Boaz live out this finely balanced relationship of *hesed* and blessing between them?

Perhaps the answer lies in examining whether the Ruth-Naomi-Boaz triad is truly polyamorous (and, as such, egalitarian) or whether Boaz, in his ability to bless, perform, and receive *hesed*, holds an unequal share of power in the relationship. Does Boaz's status within Israelite society as a wealthy male landowner (who has been traditionally assumed to be a cisgender heterosexual but may not actually be so) inherently suggest that the best that can be achieved here is a slightly less male-dominated form of polyamorous polygamy? These answers can only be addressed imaginatively. Would Boaz, who owes so much to the creativity and generosity of both Naomi and Ruth, be willing to subordinate them so completely? Does that seem to be in his character?

I believe that what I have argued thus far suggests not. Boaz, who in societal terms seems publicly to hold the most power, nevertheless employs language in Ruth 3:10 that contains a hidden transcript of his own vulnerability. If Boaz truly felt himself to be powerful, he would not have been surprised by Ruth at all. Indeed, if he felt more powerful, he might well have arranged the marriage himself, whatever his sexual preferences may have been. Instead, he says, "the last of your *hesed* is greater than the first in not going after young men whether poor or if rich." Why does he add this last part? Why should Ruth have gone after younger men? Boaz's anxiety, his hidden transcript, is breaking to the fore.

In the end, all three of them are vulnerable and must find ways to overcome their individual vulnerabilities (whether structural or emotional) in order to bless, receive *hesed*, and perform *hesed*. Insofar as may be possible—perhaps another hidden transcript is breaking out—these clues seem to expose the way in which *hesed* may underpin the resolution of the Boaz-Naomi-Ruth relationship into a polyamorous one.

NOTES

1.   יַעַשׂ ה' עִמָּכֶם חָסֶד, רַבִּי חֲנִינָא בַּר אָדָא אָמַר, יַעֲשֶׂה כְּתִיב, כַּאֲשֶׁר עֲשִׂיתָם עִם הַמֵּתִים,

שֶׁנִּטְפְּלָתֶּם בְּתַכְרִיכֵיהוֹן, וְעִמָּדִי, שֶׁוִּתְּרוּ לָהּ כְּתֻבּוֹתֵיהֶן. אָמַר

רַבִּי זְעִירָא, מְגִלָּה זוֹ אֵין בָּהּ לֹא טֻמְאָה, וְלֹא טָהֳרָה, וְלֹא

אִסּוּר, וְלֹא הֶתֵּר, וְלָמָּה נִכְתְּבָה לְלַמֶּדְךָ כַּמָּה שָׂכָר טוֹב לְגוֹמְלֵי חֲסָדִים.

2. Although the SBL academic transliteration of חסד is *ḥesed*, I will use the more common transliteration of *hesed* for this term.

3. *DCH Vol IV* ט-י, 277–81.

4. This work is Glueck's PhD dissertation, presented in 1926 and subsequently published in 1927. Norman Glueck, *Ḥesed in the Hebrew Bible*, translated by Alfred Gottschalk (Cincinnati, OH: Hebrew Union College Press, 1967).

5. Both Sakenfeld's and Clark's books are based on their PhD dissertations. Also see C. F. Whitley, "The Semantic Range of Ḥesed," *Biblica* 62, no. 4 (1981): 519–26; Hans-Jurgen Zobel, "חסד *hesed*," in *The Theological Dictionary of the Old Testament: Volume V*, edited by G. Johannes Botterweck and Helmer Ringgren (Grand Rapids, MI: William B. Eerdmans, 1986), 44–64.

6. The three instances of the use of *hesed* appear in two different sections (one as an example of secular usage between human beings and twice as examples of God's *hesed* to human beings) and both as examples of pre-exilic prose. Katherine Doob Sakenfeld, *The Meaning of Hesed in the Hebrew Bible: A New Inquiry* (Missoula, MO: Scholars Press, 1978), 42, 104, and 108.

7. Scholarly debate around the dating of the Book of Ruth continues to be divided between an early dating of the tenth/ninth centuries BCE and a post-exilic dating. See Schipper, *The Anchor Yale Bible: Ruth*, 20–22, for a summary of the current debates. Schipper himself proposes a date of at least the early Persian period (22).

8. Sakenfeld, *The Meaning of Hesed in the Hebrew Bible*, 233.

9. Sakenfeld, *The Meaning of Hesed in the Hebrew Bible*, 234.

10. Sakenfeld, *The Meaning of Hesed in the Hebrew Bible*, 234.

11. Gordon R. Clark, *The Word Hesed in the Hebrew Bible* (Sheffield: Academic Press, 1993), 37.

12. Clark, *The Word Hesed in the Hebrew Bible*, 267.

13. Clark, *The Word Hesed in the Hebrew Bible*, 267.

14. Clark, *The Word Hesed in the Hebrew Bible*, 267–68.

15. That interpersonal relationship can either be between God and human beings or between individual human beings.

16. In antiquity, the text of the Hebrew Bible was written down in consonantal form only. The vocalization of the text was preserved through oral tradition. The Masoretes, Jewish scholars of the sixth–tenth centuries CE, preserved both the vowels and the cantillation marks (chanting notations) by writing them down in codices of the

Hebrew Bible. They made no alteration to the consonantal form of the text as it had been passed down, despite in some instances a discrepancy existing between the consonantal version and the oral tradition. In these instances, the Masoretes developed a system of writing the oral tradition into the marginalia. This system became known as the *qere ketiv*, "read [and] written." Jewish communities continue to read aloud in synagogue from Torah scrolls that contain only the consonantal form of the text, nevertheless, when reading aloud, always pronounce the *qere* where these differences occur.

17. Yoo-Ki Kim, "The Agent of Ḥesed in Naomi's Blessing (Ruth 2,20)," *Biblica* 95, no. 4 (2014): 590.

18. Kim, "The Agent of Ḥesed in Naomi's Blessing," 591.

19. Kim, "The Agent of Ḥesed in Naomi's Blessing," 592–93.

20. Kim, "The Agent of Ḥesed in Naomi's Blessing," 594.

21. Kim, "The Agent of Ḥesed in Naomi's Blessing," 596.

22. Kim, "The Agent of Ḥesed in Naomi's Blessing," 596–600.

23. Kim, "The Agent of Ḥesed in Naomi's Blessing," 597.

24. Indeed, Naomi is angry with God in Ruth 1:20–21, making it harder to believe that Naomi would have felt that God should be blessed.

25. Kim, "The Agent of Ḥesed in Naomi's Blessing," 599.

26. He does not explain exactly why she might have preferred to go after a younger man, especially as he qualifies it with "whether poor or rich." We must assume, therefore, that his comment is not predominantly about wealth (though he can understand that wealth is an issue) but perhaps more fundamentally that he imagines himself to be too old for her or that, whatever their age difference, she may simply prefer someone closer in age to her.

27. See, for example, Rashi to Ruth 3:10, where he explains "the first" as "that you did for your mother-in-law."

28. Indeed, Lim states that "[t]he redactor purposely avoids placing the term *hesed* in the mouth of a recent convert from Moab." Timothy Lim, "The Book of Ruth and Its Literary Voice," in *Reflection and Refraction Studies in Biblical Historiography in Honour of A. Graeme Auld*, edited by Robert Rezetko, Timothy Lim, and Brian Auker (Leiden: Brill, 2006), 277–78, though Lim does not explain overtly why the redactor avoids doing so.

29. Orpah only displays *hesed*. She never blesses/petitions, nor is she the object of anyone's *hesed*. The dead only receive *hesed* and (self-evidently, perhaps) cannot either bless/petition or display *hesed*. Therefore, neither Orpah nor the dead are capable, in the long term, of serving as the stable, third part of the triad.

Chapter 7

Who Is Boaz?

וּלְנָעֳמִ֞י (מידע) מוֹדָ֣ע לְאִישָׁ֗הּ אִ֚ישׁ גִּבּ֣וֹר חַ֔יִל מִמִּשְׁפַּ֖חַת אֱלִימֶ֑לֶךְ וּשְׁמ֖וֹ בֹּֽעַז׃

And to Naomi there was a relation to her husband, a mighty man of valor, from the family of Elimelech and his name was Boaz. (Ruth 2:1)

Ruth 2 opens with this scene-setting verse. Notably, from the outset, Boaz is mentioned in relation to Naomi, not Ruth. Boaz is some sort of relative of Naomi. The term for describing Boaz as a relation is מודע, which is derived from a rare usage, possibly the *pual* (intensive passive) participle, of the root .ע.ד.י (*yd*ʿ), "to know."[1] He is literally, then, someone who is known to Naomi, albeit through her husband. Nevertheless, could the use of this root in this context be a subtle allusion to what is to come, or perhaps just a bit of a bawdy joke? "To know" in Biblical Hebrew is a common euphemism for sexual intercourse, which comes to imply marriage, though not one that is employed elsewhere in the Book of Ruth.[2] In Ruth 1:4, Mahlon "lifts up"—from the root .א.צ.י (*yṣ*ʾ)—Ruth, and, in Ruth 4:13, Boaz "takes"—from the root .ל.ק.ח (*lqḥ*)—Ruth and she "becomes his wife." Neither Mahlon nor Boaz "knows" Ruth, but Boaz is known to Naomi. Of course, the plain meaning of the text is that they are relations, but in the same way that the term "relations" can be used in more than one sense in English, maybe a similar double entendre is at play here.

Aside from his relationship to Naomi, this introductory verse also tells the reader that Boaz is an אִישׁ גִּבּוֹר חַיִל (ʾ*îš gibbôr ḥayil*). The term *gibbôr ḥayil* is used a number of times in the Hebrew Bible. The messenger of the Eternal One in Judg. 6:12 refers to Gideon as *gibbôr haḥayil*. The young David, as he is first introduced in 1 Sam. 16:18, is *gibbôr ḥayil*. In 1 Sam. 9:1, in introducing the young Saul, his father, Kish, is described as *gibbôr ḥayil*.

In 1 Kings 11:28, the phrase is used to describe the young Jeroboam. In 2 Kings 15:20, the term appears to describe a wealthy class of men and later, in 2 Kings 24:14, some sort of elite class. Only in 2 Chron. is the term used to denote soldiers.[3]

What are the implications of the designation for Boaz? In general, Boaz is assumed to be a *gibbôr ḥayil* not in the sense of his having any military prowess but rather as signifying someone wealthy with an elevated degree of status. Given that the text will shortly divulge that Boaz is a landowner with the clout to order around the men and women who work for him, this sense of *gibbôr ḥayil* makes most sense. Eventually, Boaz will also be depicted as a man with political nous, capable of maneuvering himself among the elders into the position of not only marrying Ruth but also gaining a piece of land in the bargain, which again fits this interpretation of *gibbôr ḥayil*.

As to the name Boaz, it may mean something like "in him is strength," though the etymology is uncertain.[4] Although the name is not used elsewhere in the Hebrew Bible as a man's proper name, Boaz is the name of one of the pillars in the portico of Solomon's Temple.[5] Despite the lack of a clear etymology, the sense of the name is clear: Boaz is something strong.[6] And, as Tod Linafelt points out, "an *allusion* does not require a precise etymology. . . . That is, the author need not have invented the name Boaz in order to make a pun or wordplay on it."[7] Clearly the Book of Ruth is playing on the idea of Boaz as a strongman, perhaps not in the literal sense but more, as Linafelt playfully suggests, in the sense of "pillar of the community."[8]

So Boaz is first a relation of Naomi, then a *gibbôr ḥayil*, and only then is he finally given a proper name. He is a man of substance, a community figure, who also happens (most crucially) to be Naomi's relative. But for all of the descriptions of Boaz, some key matters are left out. Precisely how is he related to Elimelech? Why is this towering figure unmarried? How old is he? What will his actions say about him as the story progresses? And is he really as powerful as his name suggests?

The exact nature of Boaz's relationship to Elimelech and, hence, to Naomi is never properly revealed. Boaz is described as a "relation to her husband" and "from the family of Elimelech," which potentially suggests a closer bond than appears to be the case. Boaz's ancestry is clearly laid out in the genealogy at the end of the book, but nowhere does the Hebrew Bible reveal the genealogy of Elimelech. All that the story says is that Elimelech is a man from Bethlehem (Ruth 1:1). Boaz also resides in Bethlehem, but the exact nature of the familial relationship asserted in Ruth 2:1 between the two men is impossible to determine.

Even so, early Jewish sources attempt to make clear precisely how Boaz and Elimelech are related. For example, Seder Olam Rabbah 12 states that Elimelech was the brother of Salmon and both sons of Nahshon. Salmon is

Boaz's father according to the genealogy in Ruth 4:21, thus making Boaz Elimelech's nephew. Rashi goes further in his commentary on Ruth 2:1, in which he repeats this tradition and adds that פְּלֹנִי אַלְמֹנִי (*Peloni Almoni*; the anonymous but closer kinsman in Ruth 4:1ff.) and Naomi's father are also both sons of Nahshon.[9] That would make Boaz Naomi's first cousin. These flights of rabbinic imagination might make sense of the way in which later claims in Ruth 3:9–12 state that Boaz is a redeemer and that *Peloni Almoni* is a closer relative than he is. They also suggest a general age range for Boaz— younger than Naomi but older than Ruth, most likely. But these imagined genealogies are no more than rabbinic speculation.

As for Boaz's marital status, even the Talmud is vexed by the absence of any information. According to *B. Baba Batra* 91a, Rabbi Yitzhak said, "on the same day that Ruth the Moabite came to the land of Israel, the wife of Boaz died."[10] But, of course, absolutely nothing in the biblical text suggests that Boaz has ever been married, let alone that he is a widower.

Hugh Pyper brings this issue into even sharper relief when he draws attention to the figure of the head of the reapers in Ruth 2:4–7. Pyper calls on us, as readers, to resist "heteronormative assumptions and instead attempt what we might call a homonormative reading."[11] Using this approach, Pyper goes on to ask a series of questions that turn a more traditional reading of this scene on its head. Rather than viewing Boaz's questions about the young woman reaping in his fields in heteronormative terms as a series of questions by a wealthy gentleman with his sights set on marital prospects, Pyper suggests that these questions are instead directed *at the young man*, who is the head of the reapers.

> Does his question about "who the woman belongs to" and how she came to be in the field simply reflect Boaz's interest in Ruth, or is his question prompted by his concern that the young man himself is taking an interest in her that the young man at some length tries to explain away? Is the young man's explanation of Ruth's conduct and his emphasis that she has been working without ceasing simply a generous defence of the young woman, or are there other possible readings?[12]

Moreover, Pyper further proposes that because Ruth is an ethnic Moabite, perhaps Boaz was worried about sexual licentiousness on *her* part affecting his male workers. Pyper even asks whether one of Boaz's men may have acquired Ruth in some fashion. But the real crux of Pyper's questioning is whether Ruth might be a "threat to the relationships between men in the story."[13] In other words, what really worries Boaz about his relationship with the young men who reap in his field? Is a pretty young foreign woman a threat to the homosocial relationships that Boaz has developed with his male reapers? In the end, Boaz sees to it that Ruth is removed from the company of the male reapers, by ostensibly assuring her safety in the company of other women who also reap in the fields. The biblical text makes sure that the readers understand that Boaz does so for Ruth's benefit, but could he not have been hiding his own agenda behind his actions toward her?

Again, Pyper points to other ways in which "Boaz queers the jealously guarded boundaries of the patriarchal role" to which he is assigned in the book.[14] Examining the scene on the threshing room floor in Ruth 3, Pyper states explicitly that "it definitely casts Boaz in a rather queer light."[15] This scene inverts the typical directionality in which the man looks for or exercises sexual initiative with the woman, not the other way around. Further questions arise for Pyper: What were Boaz's expectations when he went to sleep on the threshing room floor? Was he planning on a quiet night on his own, or was his surprise at being awoken caused by the fact that a woman was there? Maybe he was expecting someone else—one of the young male reapers, perhaps? Boaz knows that young men can be attractive; he says so to Ruth (Ruth 3:10). Why should readers assume that Boaz is attracted to Ruth? Perhaps he agrees to redeem her only for the land that he knows comes with the deal.[16] As Pyper says,

> The point is that readings that proceed on the basis that [Boaz] is sexually attracted to Ruth at this point are themselves based on an assumption. If we decline to follow this assumption, his subsequent permission for her to lie down at his feet could be interpreted as his indication that their relationship is companionable, not sexual.[17]

Of course, Pyper's assumptions are also based on a purely dyadic reading of the possible relationships in the text. Maybe Boaz is as open to a relationship with Ruth as he has been to one with the young men who reap in his fields. Perhaps, as a wealthy landowner, he realizes that one of these relationships need not preclude the others. As an elite male in a patriarchal society, maybe Boaz is a master of not having to choose. If so, the real question is: What does Boaz actually want out of a relationship, and with whom? Ultimately, can all of his needs really be fulfilled by a single person?

NOTES

1. Schipper, *The Anchor Yale Bible: Ruth*, 111.

2. *DCH Vol IV* ʾ – ל, 100. *ysʿ* is an extremely common root in Biblical Hebrew with a wide range of meanings. Its definition as "know a person carnally, have sexual relations [with]" is listed as its fourth meaning (out of eight). *The Theological Dictionary of the Old Testament*, while offering references to various sources as to the derivation of this meaning of the root, nevertheless concludes that "[m]ost likely we

are dealing with a euphemism for sexual relations." G. Johannes Botterwick, "יָדַ," in *TDOT Vol V* חמר – יהוה *(hmr-YHWH)*, edited by G. Johannes Botterwick and Helmer Ringgen (Grand Rapids, MI: William B. Eerdmans, 1986), 464.

3. 2 Chron. 17:13–14, 16–17; 25:6; and 32:21.

4. Schipper, *The Anchor Yale Bible: Ruth*, 113.

5. 1 Kings 7:21 and 2 Chron. 3:17. The name is not used elsewhere except in the genealogy of 1 Chron. 2:11–12, which is a version of David's genealogy.

6. Bal, for example, defines Boaz as "powerful/potent" (Mieke Bal, *Lethal Love: Feminist Literary Readings of Biblical Love Stories* [Bloomington: Indiana University Press, 1987], 75).

7. Tod Linafelt, *Berit Olam: Ruth* and *Esther* (Collegeville, MN: Liturgical Press, 1999), 25 (italics original).

8. Linafelt, *Berit Olam*, 25.

9. *pəlōnî ʾalmōnî* is the academic transliteration of this term. I will, however, use the more common *Peloni Almoni* as a quasi-proper name. In fact, the term means something more like "so and so," but as the character is never given a proper name, *Peloni Almoni* is the common way which he is referred to.

10. וְאָמַר רַבִּי יִצְחָק אוֹתוֹ הַיּוֹם שֶׁבָּאת רוּת הַמּוֹאֲבִיָּה לְאָרֶץ יִשְׂרָאֵל מֵתָה אִשְׁתּוֹ שֶׁל בֹּעַז
   Also see Ruth Rabbah 3:6.

11. Pyper, "Boaz Reawakened," 452.

12. Pyper, "Boaz Reawakened," 452.

13. Pyper, "Boaz Reawakened," 453.

14. Pyper, "Boaz Reawakened," 453.

15. Pyper, "Boaz Reawakened," 453.

16. Pyper, "Boaz Reawakened," 454–55.

17. Pyper, "Boaz Reawakened," 455.

Chapter 8

Ruth 3

What Is Romance Really?

THE SET-UP: INSTRUCTIONS (RUTH 3:1–4)

If Chapter 1 of the Book of Ruth rushes through the events of a time period spanning more than ten years and Chapter 2 focuses on the events of a single day, then Chapter 3 slows down the narrative even further, focusing on the events of a single night. As the storytelling continues to narrow in scope to this single midnight encounter, the reader is invited to concentrate not merely on the centrality of the event but also on the ways in which the account of the evening is meticulously relayed.

The episode is conveyed almost entirely through speech. Of the eighteen verses in the chapter, fourteen contain dialog, either between Naomi and Ruth (at both the beginning and the end of the chapter) or between Boaz and Ruth (in the middle of the chapter). Listening carefully to the way the three main characters talk to each other reveals much about the relationship of these characters to one another.

Naomi, deliberately described as "[Ruth's] mother-in-law," opens the chapter with a justification: "My daughter, shall I not seek for you rest that will be good for you?" First, our attention is drawn to the appellation. We know that Naomi is Ruth's mother-in-law. Why does the text remind us of that fact yet again? Naomi's first word, the one that directly follows on from חֲמוֹתָהּ (*Ḥămôtāh*), "her mother-in-law," is בִּתִּי (*Bittî*), "my daughter." The contrast is strange—mother-in-law makes more sense together with daughter-in-law, not daughter. Although the proximity of these terms could be understood as contrasting the women's positions to each other, it may equally be understood as closing the distance between them. "Mother-in-law, my daughter"—the two relational terms express that the women are bound up with each other so intimately that they are in effect bonded in the closest possible way: metaphorically, no longer affine but consanguine.

Technically, Ruth is *not* Naomi's "daughter," though in direct speech Naomi refers to Ruth as "my daughter."[1] The emphasis on these terms is deeply relational. Naomi's use of "my daughter" displays affection, but what kind of affection is what is in question here. After all, referring to Ruth as "my daughter" does not necessarily imply that Naomi views Ruth only (or even primarily) as a daughter. Indeed, Boaz, too, consistently refers to Ruth as "my daughter" (Ruth 2:8; 3:10–11).[2] Instead, "my daughter" should be understood as a term of affection and, from its context here in the Book of Ruth, one that clearly transcended parental feelings.[3]

As for Naomi's opening gambit, she expresses a need to explain what she is about to tell Ruth to do. Unlike Ruth, who at the start of Chapter 2 asks Naomi for permission, Naomi will be instructing Ruth with the expectation that Ruth will obey her. Naomi does not ask for permission but rather seeks, at least, to elucidate her instructions. If Ruth is concerned about looking for favor in the eyes of a man, Naomi is clearly anxious that sending Ruth out to seduce one into marriage will place even more strain on Naomi and Ruth's relationship to each other. "Shall I not seek for you,"—that is, "What else can I do/the only the responsible thing for me to do is . . ." Naomi might have put her words more positively, but instead she employs the negative interrogative particle הֲלֹא (*Hălō'*). Her syntax is a question, and yet she is not really asking a question; rather, her speech conveys a sort of plaintive plea for understanding. Naomi seeks rest and happiness for Ruth and, in so doing, implies that, much as Naomi may wish that the two women were at rest and happy with just each other, they are not complete. Ruth cannot find rest and happiness with Naomi, or at least not with Naomi alone. As if to further underline this point, Naomi refers to Boaz as מֹדַעְתָּנוּ (*Mōda'tānû*), "one who is known to *us*" (i.e., *our* kinsman).[4] He is neither the close relation nor the redeemer of Ruth 2:20; rather, here is a possible pun. Boaz could perhaps be someone who could be carnally "known" to both women, allowing them to retain their own relationship while bringing Boaz in, too.

Alternatively—or, indeed, in addition to that reading—verse 1 suggests the possibility that Naomi is expressing a degree of compersion. Compersion is a modern term used predominantly in polyamorous communities, which describes the feeling of taking delight in someone else's happiness, particularly regarding romantic and/or sexual fulfillment. Compersion, therefore, is the opposite of jealousy.[5] Naomi's *hălō'* would then mean something more like "Why shouldn't I seek rest for you, where you will be happy?" with the implication that Ruth has nothing to fear from being happy with a man (as well). Far from a relationship with a man potentially threatening or interfering with Naomi's relationship with Ruth, she may be encoding that not only

does Naomi seek what is good, or best, for Ruth, but she, too, will find pleasure in it. Ruth's good fortune will be Naomi's as well. In polyamorous relationships, this ability to feel compersion enables happier, better-functioning
relationships among all parties because they can enjoy the pleasure that each
of them takes in each other without the damaging effects of jealousy.

Perhaps in this situation, *hesed* might also be linked to compersion. If
hesed is "an emotion that leads to an activity beneficial to the recipient . . .
in the context of a deep and enduring commitment between two persons or
parties," then surely compersion is an emotion that achieves precisely such
benefit within the context of enduring commitment between people.[6] Here,
Naomi and Ruth have a relationship of "deep and enduring commitment," and
Naomi's expressed desire to find happiness for Ruth will lead to "an activity
beneficial" to Ruth. Understood in this fashion, *hesed*/compersion will help
form the necessary building blocks for a healthy polyamorous relationship.

So, knowing that Ruth, too, understands that she must find favor in the eyes
of a man, Naomi reminds her of Boaz, as though Ruth had somehow forgotten about him. Nowhere is the hidden transcript of the triadic relationship
between Ruth, Boaz, and Naomi more evident than in the following verses.
On two separate occasions in verses 3–4, Naomi appears to insert herself into
(what will be) the threshing room floor scene. As Naomi instructs Ruth on
what she must do, Naomi begins by telling Ruth to wash, anoint herself, and
dress up, but just at the point when Naomi is about to tell Ruth to go down to
the threshing room, the text contains *qere ketiv*.[7] The written text (*ketiv*) states
that *Naomi* will go down to the threshing room floor—וירדתי (*wəyarādti*; first-
person singular)—not Ruth. But when read aloud (*qere*), the text is vocalized
as וְיָרַדְתְּ (*wəyāradt*), in keeping with the rest of the verbs in verse 3 (which
are second-person feminine singular), so that the listener always hears the
instruction that *Ruth* should go down.[8]

Perhaps even more interestingly, in verse 4, Naomi further instructs
Ruth to keep track of Boaz, to note where he lies down to sleep, and then
to uncover something—perhaps herself, perhaps part of Boaz's body (the
Hebrew is ambiguous). But again, at this point, the text contains a *qere ketiv*,
as Naomi employs the first person instead of the second person. According to
the *ketiv*, Naomi says, ושכבתי (*wəsakāābt*), "and I will lie down" (as opposed
to the *qere*, וְשָׁכָבְתְּ (*wəsākābət*; "you will lie down"). So, who is to go down
to the threshing room floor and perform this late-night seduction—Naomi or
Ruth? Both at the point of going down to the threshing room floor *and* at the
point of actually lying down, the text contains verbal ambiguity, or fluidity.
Either Naomi is instructing Ruth to do these things or, in some fashion, she
imagines that she is doing them herself.

The preservation of the *qere ketiv* allows slippage between the two possibilities and, thus, allows readers a possible glimpse into Naomi's inner

thoughts.[9] Is Naomi so close to Ruth that she almost imagines herself and Ruth as a sort of single entity? Perhaps, too, although in Ruth 1:11 Naomi tells Ruth and Orpah that she is no longer fertile, that does not mean that she is no longer a sexual being with desires. Could Naomi have actually imagined herself in these moments, rendering these *qere ketiv* Freudian slips? Perhaps she wished to seduce Boaz herself because she can imagine a scenario in which she, Naomi, remarries and creates a new home into which Ruth might be brought and be safe. Boaz could have accepted Ruth as his daughter in earnest then and arranged a marriage for her (with someone closer to her own age, for example). But such daydreams cannot be realized. Naomi understands that the midnight seductress must be someone capable of bearing children for Boaz, or else, she may have worried, there would be little motivation for marriage. Alternatively, perhaps Naomi just thinks that Boaz would prefer the young, fertile Ruth to her past-her-prime self. As all of these thoughts pass through her head while she speaks, her tongue simply reveals her inner conflict, and the text is left with these traces of Naomi's turmoil in the form of incongruous verbs.

If we, however, accept the possibility of Naomi as Ruth's lover, Naomi's slip of the tongue could have a different import. Naomi has already accepted in her head, first, that this seduction must happen to ensure their joint futures and, second, that only Ruth can enact the seduction. Naomi nevertheless wants to reassure Ruth somehow, to let her know that she, Naomi, will be with Ruth, in spirit if not in flesh. In allowing her speech to slide between first and second person, Naomi's Freudian slip becomes an act of solidarity, of being present with Ruth. Rather than casting Ruth out to form a new, heteropatriarchal relationship in which Naomi may have little (if any) involvement, Naomi is signaling a desire to be part of what happens next, even if she cannot actually be there in person.[10]

Considering this scene through a polyamorous hermeneutic, these *qere ketiv* present yet another possibility. Perhaps Naomi might have actually intended "to go down" and "to lie down" herself on the threshing room floor alongside Ruth. Might Naomi be telling Ruth to make herself ready and get Boaz in the mood, but/and she, Naomi, is intending to join in as well? As will be made clear in verses 6–14, the text does not relate that Naomi was, in the end, physically present in the scene, but neither does that preclude the prospect that in her own mind, at least, it was her intention. The shift between the first person and the second person in verses 3–4 would, in such a scenario, be far more intentional and not a slip at all, but rather a subversive means of communicating an intention to create a polyamorous union.

I want to acknowledge that the most straightforward explanation for the *qere ketiv* is, simply, a scribal error or textual corruption and that Naomi's tongue never slipped at all. Nevertheless, the interpretative possibilities of the *qere ketiv* should not be overlooked or minimized. The classical rabbinic interpretative mode often rests on flights of imagination far less rooted in the plain meaning of the text than this one.[11] In preserving the *qere ketiv*, the Hebrew Bible gifts the reader a textually based opportunity to imagine the meaning of Naomi's words differently.

Yet I also want to acknowledge that the traditional enactment of the *qere ketiv* has silenced and sanitized the fractured nature of the text. In only ever reading aloud and in only privileging the "corrected" version of the text, many never fathom what is *actually written* in the text. Additionally, the choice to translate only the *qere* means that many never encounter the *ketiv* at all.[12] This silencing has meant that the potentialities of Naomi's speech have not been explored properly, including (as I have pointed out) the possibility of a polyamorous reading of the text.

Beyond the *qere ketiv*, verses 3–4 tell us much about Naomi's ability to strategize and Ruth's need for someone to give her instruction. The two women might have considered waiting for Boaz to make a move. Surely that was at the root of Ruth's request in Ruth 2:2, her hope that she would find favor in some man's eyes. But either the process was not moving along speedily enough or, as Pyper suggests, Boaz was never going to move the process along proactively because he was primarily interested in homonormative relationships and his concern for Ruth was only ever a general sort of kindness. Naomi, however, may be feeling that if Ruth (and, by extension, she herself) were ever going to secure a socially acceptable and financially stable future, she would need to devise a plan and instruct Ruth in it. Naomi demonstrates clarity of thought, care for Ruth, and good organizational acumen. And, as the narrative will confirm, her plan is sensible and, ultimately, successful.

Yet from the outset of Naomi's instructions, questions arise. Why does Naomi need to tell Ruth to make herself look and smell presentable? Are Ruth and Naomi, between themselves, so comfortable with each other and so used to the deprivations of life that they no longer need to beautify themselves for each other's sake? Moreover, ought not Ruth know how to make herself attractive to a man, given that she was married to one for some ten years? Perhaps the need for these instructions hints again at the possibility that Ruth's marriage to Mahlon was never consummated.[13]

The core of the plan, however, is that Ruth should wait for Boaz to finish eating and drinking before noting where he lies down for the night. Satiated, half asleep, and likely intoxicated, Boaz would be far more pliable than when sober in the full light of day. Clearly, Naomi recognizes that Boaz needs to be in a susceptible state in order to be approached, suggesting that however much *hesed* he may have shown Ruth, Naomi does not think it will extend to marriage (at least not without a little nudge!). Boaz does not just need a push;

he needs a push when he is especially exposed in order to do something that many (if not most) men in his position might have understood as obvious. In Boaz, Naomi spots a fellow traveler off the beaten heteropatriarchal path and seeks to exploit that vulnerability in him.[14]

After marking out where Boaz lies down, Ruth is to go over to him and וְגִלִּית מַרְגְּלֹתָיו (*wəgillît margəlōtāyw*).[15] The precise meaning of this phrase is contested. The noun רֶגֶל (*regel*) means "foot," or sometimes "leg," but may also be a euphemism for the genitals.[16] Moreover, the locative מ suggests that rather than Ruth uncovering Boaz's "feet," Naomi may be instructing Ruth to uncover herself at the place of Boaz's "feet."[17] After this act of uncovering, Ruth is to lie down and await instructions from Boaz. Although exactly what Ruth is uncovering remains obscure, the thrust of what she is to do is clear. Ruth is to place herself in a compromising position with Boaz in order to goad him into marriage. Naomi is instructing Ruth deliberately to place herself in a precarious and potentially dangerous situation in the hope that Boaz will "do the right thing."

THE SET-UP: CONSENT (RUTH 3:5)

In verse 5, Ruth's response is brief: כֹּל אֲשֶׁר־תֹּאמְרִי (אֵלַי) אֶעֱשֶׂה (*kōl ʾăšer-tōʾmrî [ʾēlai] ʾeʿĕśeh*), "Everything you will say [to me], I will do."[18] The text gives us no emotional clues to Ruth's motivation in this response, but the clues are hidden throughout the previous chapters. Ruth's actions up to now—her declaration to Naomi in Ruth 1:16–17, her deference to Naomi in Ruth 2:2, her bringing back food to Naomi in chapter 2—all point toward Ruth's unswerving commitment to and trust in Naomi. What is most important about Ruth's reply, however, is that it exists and is recorded. Her response to Naomi's instruction reads distinctly as an expression of consent.

Although Ruth's reply, *kōl ʾăšer-tōʾmrî (ʾēlai) ʾeʿĕśeh*, is more commonly translated as something like "She replied, 'I will do everything you tell me'" (NJPS), both verbs are actually imperfects. Although "everything you will say to me, I will do" is more awkward in English, I believe this translation more accurately describes Ruth's response. Ruth is intimating that everything Naomi will *ever* ask of her, she will *always* do. This sense of ongoing consent to what Naomi asks suggests a level of substantial trust between Ruth and Naomi, which further reinforces Ruth's profound commitment to Naomi.

If Ruth continues to be fully committed to Naomi, can the reverse be inferred from the text as well? Although Naomi does not respond to Ruth's declaration in Ruth 1:16–17, both in Chapter 2 and here in Chapter 3, Naomi's direct speech suggests something more than the resignation relayed in Ruth 1:18. In Ruth 2:22, Naomi displays regard for Ruth's well-being. Here

Naomi's qualification of what she is asking Ruth to do also suggests that in framing her opening remarks in Ruth 3:2 with the interrogative *hălō*ʾ, Naomi may be trying to give some space for Ruth to respond, to exercise some degree of choice, and thereby consent.

The subject of consent in the Hebrew Bible is contentious. Within its heteropatriarchal world, the concept of women's consent to marriage hardly exists. Aside from one notable exception—Gen. 24:58, when Rebekah is asked directly whether she will go with Abraham's servant (in order to be married to Isaac), she says, "I will"—the text does not mention whether women have any say in their marital arrangements.[19] Yet much of the discussion around consent in the Hebrew Bible centers not on marital choice per se, but rather on debates around rape and consensual sex.[20]

Recently, Rhiannon Graybill has written extensively on the subject of consent in *Texts After Terror: Rape, Sexual Violence, and the Hebrew Bible*.[21] Graybill problematizes the subject:

> Consent discourses flatten and erase the fuzzy, the messy, and the icky. They impose anachronistic and, more importantly, antifeminist notions of the liberal subject onto ancient texts. They ignore discomfort and subtle forms of coercion. They neglect race, ethnicity, and other questions of intersectionality and risk slipping into a colonialist project of saving women. They legitimize subordination. And they set too low a bar, foreclosing questions of pleasure. And yet, we also have alternatives.[22]

So in using the term "consent" here, I want to acknowledge all of the possible "fuzzy, messy, and icky" "edges of consent" that exist between Ruth and Naomi.[23] Ruth is ethnically a Moabite, as opposed to Naomi, who is an Israelite, which within the world of the story makes Ruth foreign and Naomi indigenous. Ruth is subordinate to Naomi as the older woman and her mother-in-law. Yet Ruth is potentially fertile, whereas Naomi is ostensibly beyond childbearing age. Ruth might well be "in love" with Naomi, who may or may not reciprocate her feelings. All of these matters lend to a range of power dynamics between them, making the boundaries of their relationship unclear, often complicated, and sometimes uncomfortable. As readers, we are left to make our own judgments about Naomi's intentions and Ruth's understanding of them.

Nevertheless, between Ruth and Naomi as they relate to each other within these constraints of the heteropatriarchal world that they inhabit, Ruth finds her own voice, both here and previously, to state clearly that she will follow Naomi. Her choice to do so may have been constrained by any number of factors, and yet on each occasion when Ruth's commitment could have been in question, she reiterates, in some form, her pledge to Naomi. Ruth might simply not have replied at all (much like Naomi in Ruth 1:18) while still carrying out Naomi's plans. That would have been a different kind of choice. Instead, Ruth *does* reply, *does* speak, and *does* agree to do what Naomi requests. Ruth has already expressed her own desires (Ruth 1:16–17) in following Naomi back to Bethlehem. Now she speaks again and extends her consent to following Naomi once more, even if that leads to marriage with a man. In this fashion, and with all these considerations in mind, we can begin to see the shape of a consensual polyamorous relationship beginning to unfold.

SPRINGING THE TRAP: THE ENCOUNTER IN THE NIGHT (RUTH 3:6–15A)

In verses 6–7, Ruth follows Naomi's plan—up to a point. Ruth goes to the threshing room floor and does precisely as instructed. Boaz, unwittingly, also follows the script when he eats and drinks, and "his heart was happy"—that is, he was satiated and drunk. He lies down, and Ruth uncovers something (either herself or his "feet") and lies down beside him. The set-up is now complete.

In verse 8, the trap is sprung, but Boaz's immediate response is not what one might expect from a heteronormative male in a patriarchal society.[24] The end of the verse—"He was grasped and behold a woman was lying at the place of his feet"—demonstrates that Boaz's surprise stems particularly from a *woman* lying at his feet. Naomi seems to have been correct in identifying that for Boaz, a woman at his side is unexpected—hence the need to manipulate the situation.[25] In verse 9, half asleep and possibly still inebriated, Boaz is unable to determine who is lying beside him. Not only is he confused in his sleepy stupor, but he obviously does not anticipate Ruth to be lying at his feet (if, indeed, he was anticipating anyone at all).

At this point, Ruth improvises and diverges from Naomi's instructions. Boaz wants to know who is lying at his feet. Ruth could have stopped at "I am Ruth, your maidservant." Instead, she embellishes her reply by requesting that Boaz spread his wing over her—suggesting that she is the one uncovered—and points out to him that he is a גֹּאֵל (*Gōʾēl*), a redeemer.[26] Naomi apprised Ruth of this essential information in Ruth 2:20, but she certainly did not tell Ruth to use this language with Boaz. Naomi only told Ruth to wait for Boaz's directions. Perhaps Naomi did not realize just how shocked Boaz would be by Ruth's presence, thinking that even a man with tendencies toward more homosocial relationships would understand the expectations of heteropatriarchal society in the circumstances that she had helped engineer. Ruth has the presence of mind to remind Boaz of his position and responsibility (or duty), which he apparently has not yet grasped, let alone acted on.

Boaz, now more (literally and figuratively) awake to his obligations, replies to Ruth in verse 10. He makes a virtue of Ruth's unexpected (and what could easily have been read as problematic) behavior. According to Boaz, Ruth has acted with *hesed* because she could have gone after younger men, whatever their financial status. Instead of either taking advantage of Ruth—it is dark and she is a foreigner—or throwing her out, he tells her in verse 12 that he is not the closest redeemer to her after all. He chooses to see Ruth in the best possible light. He does not ask why she thought to come to him in this peculiar fashion; rather, his first thought is that she has behaved with some sort of generosity toward him. This is not the most immediately obvious thing for her to have taken, nor is it the most obvious way for him to respond. But Boaz nonetheless frames this night-time sort of seduction as an act of Ruth's generosity and kindness, to which he ought to respond with similar generosity and kindness, almost as if he is using a sort of "coded" polyamorous language.

Moreover, while referring to Ruth's action as *hesed*, he explicitly connects it to her previous act of *hesed*. The only explicitly mentioned previous act of *hesed* on Ruth's part is in Ruth 1:8, in which Naomi commends both Ruth and Orpah for the *hesed* with which they have treated both herself and the dead. Is this the act of *hesed* to which Boaz is referring, or does he believe, more generally, that Ruth's return with Naomi to Bethlehem and her care for and commitment to Naomi throughout this period constitute as an act of *hesed*? Although the head of the reapers tells Boaz in Ruth 2:6 that Ruth is the woman who returned with Naomi from Moab, at no point does this young man (or anyone else) tell Boaz that Ruth's return with Naomi is an act of *hesed*. This judgment is one he makes on his own.

In connecting Ruth's *hesed* toward Naomi with her *hesed* toward him, Boaz is connecting the unexpected ways that Ruth cuts across the normative boundaries of Israelite society. Both Boaz and Naomi are older than Ruth, which Boaz emphasizes in praising Ruth for not pursuing a younger man. Both Boaz and Naomi are in need of a relationship—Naomi, because she is a childless widow, and Boaz, because he is unmarried (and, apparently, also without offspring). Ruth has already committed herself to Naomi, ensuring that Naomi has someone with whom she can go through life; now Ruth is offering to do the same for Boaz.

But as Boaz has already acknowledged that Ruth has acted with *hesed* toward Naomi in standing by her, he must also understand from this first moment that Ruth cannot and will not simply stop behaving with *hesed* to Naomi just because she is now offering to do the same for him. Indeed, he may actually be signaling that he expects Ruth to continue to act with *hesed* toward Naomi. Alongside his comment regarding younger men, Boaz is subtly alluding to understanding the situation clearly; Ruth's *hesed* will glue the three of them together.

Boaz's response in verse 11 is no surprise. He reassures Ruth, telling her not to fear, that he will do what she asks of him, and that everyone knows that she is an אֵשֶׁת חַיִל (*ʾēšeṯ ḥayil*), "a woman of valor." This expression is another key to unlocking Boaz's point of view. Boaz is described in Ruth 2:1 as a *gibbôr ḥayil*, and the use of the term *ḥayil* marks them out as complementary to each other. In Ruth, Boaz recognizes someone who corresponds to himself.

The appellation *ʾēšeṯ ḥayil* has a particular resonance through the poem at the end of the Book of Proverbs (Prov. 31:10ff.) and, in some configurations of the canon, immediately preceding the Book of Ruth.[27] An *ʾēšeṯ ḥayil* is here described in considerable detail, but, crucially, she is not portrayed as sexualized in any fashion. In fact, Prov. 31:30 clearly states that שֶׁקֶר הַחֵן וְהֶבֶל הַיֹּפִי (*šeqer haḥēn wǝheḇel hayyōp̄î*), "Grace is deceitful and beauty vapid"—in other words, do not trust sexual allure.[28] Instead, the *ʾēšeṯ ḥayil* is a kind of superwoman who does everything practical to ensure the well-being of her household, skills that Ruth might well have learned from Naomi during their ten years of keeping house together in Moab. The husband of an *ʾēšeṯ ḥayil* is left free to sit at the gates of the city with the elders (Prov. 31:23), much as Boaz will do in Chapter 4.

Despite telling Ruth that he will do whatever she asks of him, Boaz also reveals the spanner in the works of the plot: although he is a redeemer, another, closer kinsman exists. How could Naomi have forgotten this detail? Did she only send Ruth to Boaz because Ruth had, by chance, already been gleaning in his field and had established a bond? Or does Naomi believe that where Boaz may be open to a less traditional relationship (polyamorous, crossing ethnic boundaries, etc.), the unnamed closer kinsman would not? Moreover, why is this plot twist needed at all? Surely, the text could simply have dispensed with the entirety of this plotline and skipped straight over to Boaz taking Ruth as his wife. Why shoehorn in the convoluted and problematic section on redeemers and levirate marriage? (I will return to these questions in the following chapter.)

Returning to Boaz's speech in verse 13, he tells Ruth that if the closer kinsman wishes to redeem her, then that will happen, but if this kinsman does *not* wish to redeem her, then Boaz swears that, as the Eternal One lives, he will come to her aid. In fact, his statement is far from reassuring. If Ruth and Naomi had been intent on Boaz marrying Ruth, then the possibility of this closer kinsman doing so instead poses an element of risk and would not be the desired outcome. Ruth could end up in a marriage with someone she does not know at all and whose demeanor toward her is yet to be established. Boaz is not *so* excited by the prospect of marriage to Ruth that he leaps at the offer; rather, he hedges around, appearing ambivalent, both resistant and supportive at the same time.

In Boaz's final comment to Ruth, he tells her to remain lying by him until morning. Why? Would Ruth not have been safer leaving under the cover of darkness? Boaz has spoken fine words to Ruth and let her know that he may not, after all, be able to marry her. The text is clear that Boaz was not expecting Ruth to be there at all, and we may suspect that he was expecting someone else—perhaps one of the male reapers. Yet in asking Ruth to stay the rest of the night, possibly uncovered by his lower body, he is inviting sustained physical contact between them. Full, penetrative sexual intercourse need not have occurred (particularly not if he were more accustomed to same-sex relations) for them to have explored enjoyment of each other's physical presence. In doing so, they might have been able to establish some type of companionable, mutually beneficial physical intimacy.

THE RETURN TO NAOMI (AGAIN; RUTH 3:15B–18)

At the end of Chapter 2, Ruth returns to Naomi after her encounter with Boaz, and so, too, she does here, at the end of Chapter 3, after her more charged encounter with Boaz. Ruth rises early in the morning—probably, by the description, just before dawn. The phrase יַכִּיר אִישׁ אֶת־רֵעֵהוּ (*yakkîr 'îš 'et̲-rē 'ēhû*), "before a man will recognize his friend," is curious given the context. This time of the early morning would obscure Ruth's exit altogether, but, equally, if Boaz's young men were expecting to see one of their own leaving Boaz's side, then being unable "to recognize one's own friend" would enable them to see just what they expected to see. Furthermore, Boaz goes on to express his concern about anyone discovering that the woman had been on the threshing room floor with him. Although normally taken to mean that he is concerned that people would know that Ruth had been there with him, the text could equally mean that he was concerned that people would know that a *woman* had been with him. Again, this concern could reflect a desire to protect Ruth as much as it could allude to his own homosocial relations. What would his male reapers think if they found out that a woman, but perhaps particularly *this* woman, to whom he had already behaved so generously, had been with him all night?

NOTES

1. Ruth 1:11, 13 (plural includes Orpah); 2:2, 22; 3:16 and 18.
2. Cf. Kandy Queen-Sutherland, *Ruth and Esther* (Macon, GA: Smyth and Helwys, 2016), 88: "by using the nomenclature 'my daughter,' Boaz signals that Ruth is moving from Naomi's sphere of influence—Naomi having called Ruth 'my daughter' in 2:2 in sending her off to the fields—to Boaz's sphere." An alternative

explanation could be that both Naomi and Boaz have a similar degree and type of affection for Ruth that warrants the use of this term.

3. *Bittî* used in direct speech to the girl/woman in question is only used here in Ruth and once in Judg. 11:35, when Jephthah talks directly to his daughter. Elsewhere, the term in used to talk about someone's daughter, but not to her. We do not have enough data from elsewhere in the Hebrew Bible, therefore, to discern how else the term might have been used.

Cf. Cant 4:9, 10, 12; 5:1, where the male lover uses the phrase "my sister, my bride" in relation to his female lover. The term here is אֲחֹתִי [*'ăḥōṯî*], meaning sister, not daughter, but the usage could, perhaps, similarly denote romantic endearment.

4. See note 2 in the previous chapter, "Who Is Boaz?"

5. For example, Ben Ze'ev: "Compersion is the feeling of being happy for your partner's romantic affair with someone else. As such, compersion is a form of sympathetic joy. Compersion falls on the opposite end of the spectrum to jealousy." Aaron Ben Ze'ev, "'I Am Glad That My Partner Is Happy with Her Lover': On Jealousy and Compersion," in *The Moral Psychology of Love*, edited by Arina Pismenny and Berit Bogaard (Lanham, MD: Rowman & Littlefield, 2022), 130.

6. Clark, *The Word Hesed in the Hebrew Bible*, 267.

7. See note 16 in chapter 6, "חסד *Hesed*: An Excursus," for an explanation of the *qere ketiv*.

8. Cf. Wendy Doniger, *The Bedtrick: Tales of Sex and Masquerade* (Chicago: University of Chicago Press, 2000), 261.

9. I want to thank and acknowledge one of my former students, Daniel Vulcan, who, many years ago, imaginatively translated these verses in our megillot class in a way that more clearly brought out the Freudian slip possibilities to me.

10. Contra Gafney, "Mother Knows Best," 31, who sees this section of the story as an evidence of Naomi's sexploitation of Ruth.

11. For example, rabbinic hermeneutics allow for the revocalization of words, inversions of letters to create new meanings, and gematria (where numerical values are assigned to the Hebrew alphabet and words with the same numerical value can be associated with each other to create interpretations).

12. For example, see https://www.biblegateway.com/verse/en/Ruth%203:3 for a comparison of a large number of English language translations. None of them even hint that there is any textual problem in this verse. Even in the NJPS, one must have facility with the Hebrew text, including training to understand how textual emendations function, in order to understand the textual problem here.

13. Or only just consummated as per the requirements to consider the marriage valid, but nothing that required any actual seduction on Ruth's part. Or, as per Gafney, it may have been a "rape-marriage," which certainly would not have involved any seduction.

14. Alternatively or additionally, Naomi may have felt that because Ruth was a Moabite, Boaz had not yet or would not have been inclined to think of Ruth as a potential marriage partner.

15. NJPS, NRSV, and NIV all translate "uncover his feet." By way of comparison, NET translates "uncover his legs" and NABRE "uncover a place at his feet."

16. *DCH Vol VII* צ-ר, 411.

17. See Schipper, *The Anchor Yale Bible: Ruth*, 143–44, for a more extensive discussion of these points.

18. ʾēlai, "to me," is a *qere* (but not *ketiv*). The insertion or not of "to me" makes little substantive difference to the overall meaning.

19. Even Michal, who is presented as in love with David, does not have a spoken line in which she consents to marry him. Rather, the text presents her as a young woman in love who is passed from her father, King Saul, to David as a political pawn.

20. Beginning in the 1980s, feminist scholars, in particular, began to investigate, analyze, comment on, and challenge the stories of rape in the biblical text (i.e., the stories of Dinah, Tamar [2 Sam. 13:1–22], the women of Shiloh and Jabesh-gilead, the Levite's secondary wife, etc.) and, in doing so, address the issue of consent, both overtly and implicitly, in the Hebrew Bible. See, for example, Bal, "The Rape of Narrative and Narrative of Rape"; Caroline Blyth, *The Narrative of Rape in Genesis 34: Interpreting Dinah's Silence* (Oxford: Oxford University Press, 2010); J. Cheryl Exum, *Fragmented Women: Feminist (Sub)versions of Biblical Narrative* (London: Bloomsbury, T&T Clark, 1993/2015); Robert Kawashima, "Could A Woman Say 'No' in Biblical Israel? On the Genealogy of Legal Status in Biblical Law and Literature," *Association for Jewish Studies Review* 35 (2011): 1–22; Helen Paynter, *Telling Terror in Judges 19: Rape and Reparation for the Levite's Wife* (London: Routledge, 2020); Susanne Scholz, *Sacred Witness: Rape in the Hebrew Bible* (Minneapolis, MN: Fortress, 2010); Phyllis Trible, *God and the Rhetoric of Sexuality* (Philadelphia: Fortress Press, 1978); Renita J. Weems, *Battered Love: Marriage, Sex, and Violence in the Hebrew Prophets* (Minneapolis, MN: Fortress, 1995); and Frank Yamada, *Configurations of Rape in the Hebrew Bible: A Literary Analysis of Three Rape Narratives* (New York: Peter Lang, 2008). For a more extensive bibliography, see https://www.shilohproject.blog/resources/.

21. Rhiannon Graybill, *Texts After Terror: Rape Sexual Violence, and the Hebrew Bible* (Oxford: Oxford University Press, 2021).

22. Graybill, *Texts After Terror*, 57.

23. Graybill, *Texts After Terror*, 30.

24. See the previous chapter.

25. Cf. Doniger, *The Bedtrick*, 259.

26. Cf. Laura Quick, *Dress, Adornment and the Body in the Hebrew Bible* (Oxford: Oxford University Press, 2021), 39–41. Quick argues that, in fact, Ruth's speech is not an embellishment at all, but rather a form of technical language designed to invite Boaz to marry her.

27. See note 3 in chapter 1, "The Setting."

28. Interestingly, and perhaps tellingly, neither Boaz nor the narrator (nor Naomi, for that matter) ever describe Ruth as beautiful. Whereas other female biblical women, such as Sarah (Gen. 12:11, "pleasing to look at"), Rachel (Gen. 29:17, "beautiful shape and pleasing to look at"), and Esther (Esther 2:7, "beautiful shape and good looking"), are described in terms of their physical appearance, Ruth never is, which suggests that her character is what is most important about her.

Chapter 9

Ruth 4

Dyadic or Triadic: What Does Happily Ever After Actually Look Like?

LEVIRATE MARRIAGE OR REDEEMER:
THE SUBPLOT (RUTH 4:1–13)

Unlike Chapters 2 and 3, Chapter 4 of the Book of Ruth begins, like Chapter 1, by moving the action away from the world of women back to the world of men. But unlike Chapter 1, which only briefly suggests a regular, heteronormative story and then moves off rapidly in another direction, the largest section of Chapter 4 focuses determinedly on heteropatriarchal matters. Superficially at least, this story redirects the reader away from Ruth and Naomi as figures with autonomous agency, inner lives, and independent voices, toward Ruth as little more than chattel to be negotiated on and passed between men. Yet away from the surface of the story lie oblique pointers to what else may be hiding beneath.

The action opens in verse 1, with Boaz going to the gates of the city to sit down and await his opportunity. Opportunity passes by within the very same verse: וַיֵּשֶׁב שָׁם וְהִנֵּה הַגֹּאֵל עֹבֵר (*wayyēšeb̠ šām wəhinnēh haggō'ēl 'ōb̠ēr*), "he [Boaz] sat there and, behold, the redeemer passed by." In verse 2, Boaz calls this redeemer, the generically named *Peloni Almoni*, over to sit and then arranges for ten more male elders of the city to come sit with them as well.[1] With witnesses in place, the negotiations can start in earnest. This all-male group will decide the future of the women who have hitherto been the driving ˙rs of the story. Unpicking the motivations of these men, particularly of ˙nd *Peloni Almoni*, is hampered by a number of textual factors, includ- ˙cise grammar, an apparent conflation of biblical legal practices, and ˙nae.

˙-7, the text recounts a convoluted dialog between Boaz and ˙Beginning in verse 3, Boaz introduces the problem of an agricultural field that belongs, apparently, to Naomi and that she is in the process of selling it. In addition to the thorny question of whether (or at least to what extent) a woman in this period could own property, this field has never been mentioned before in the story.[2] According to Boaz, the field was the property of Elimelech and hence, by implication, was inherited by Naomi, who has the right to sell it off. When did Boaz become aware of the issue of this field? How does he know that Naomi wishes to sell it? Why doesn't Boaz mention the field as part of the situation that requires negotiation when he speaks to Ruth on the threshing room floor (Chapter 3)? Why does he choose to raise the subject now with *Peloni Almoni*, when the reader has been led to believe that Boaz will be discussing the subject of marriage to Ruth?

Commentators, both ancient and modern, provide much speculation over how Boaz knows about this field. Given that Naomi (and, by extension, Ruth) does not appear to benefit from this field and the women are reduced to gleaning in order to survive, the general view is that Elimelech must have, in some fashion, sold or leased the land or its usufruct before he departed for Moab. In the light of Naomi's return from Moab as his widow, she seeks to buy the land back and return it to the control of the family, but lacks the means to do so.[3] Perhaps, however, the field simply lies fallow after years of lack of use, and by the time of Naomi and Ruth's return to Bethlehem, it is too late in the season to plant it for productive use. Perhaps, in the longer term, the two women could not have dealt with the field on their own. Whatever the case, the field has suddenly sprung into existence in the story.

So how did Boaz know about it? In my commentary at the end of chapter 2, I discuss an ambiguous passage of time with no description in the text of what has happened during that interval. One obvious possibility is that the characters encountered each other in situations that the narrator chose not to recount. Perhaps the assumption is that these encounters were obvious to the reader and that some of them would have, in any case, been implied by other elements in the story. In that regard, the possibility that Boaz spoke with the widow of his deceased kinsman to pay respects, to check on her well-being, and to offer support seems entirely plausible. Yet largely unremarked on by commentators is the fact that in the whole of the Book of Ruth, Boaz and Naomi are *never* presented as directly interacting.[4] In a book so heavily reliant on direct speech and with only three main characters, two of these characters, Naomi and Boaz, are never described as speaking to each other.

This lacuna in the text can and should raise suspicions. What is being kept out of the story is as interesting as what is included. Boaz knows information—in this case, about Naomi's field—for which the most obvious source is Naomi herself, and yet nowhere is he overtly described as communicating with her. How could Boaz purport to speak *for* Naomi when, apparently, he has never spoken *with* her?[5] He clearly knows that Naomi is back in

Bethlehem and that Naomi's widowed daughter-in-law is gleaning in his fields. Would he simply have ignored Naomi during this period? More likely, he did have some contact with her, and she surely would have mentioned the business of her field to him. Nothing more convoluted than an entirely probable conversation between two relatives explains how Boaz knew about the field and Naomi's need to sell it. Hence, he was able to raise the matter with *Peloni Almoni.*

But why would such a conversation have gone unreported by the narrator? What would have been at risk if the narrator had described Boaz and Naomi encountering each other? If the central drive of Chapters 2 and 3 is to establish a link between Ruth and Boaz that will lead to marriage, then perhaps the concern is that a conversation between Boaz and *Naomi* may have undermined or complicated that plot line. Yet if we are searching for any hint, however oblique, for the establishment of a polyamorous family, then surely here is a clue: the possibility of Boaz and Naomi communicating about property and the need to redeem it for the benefit of all three of them.

Nevertheless, in raising the issue of the field in the way he does, Boaz appears to be enacting a high-risk strategy for his conversation with *Peloni Almoni.* What if *Peloni Almoni*'s desire for the field had been sufficient motivation for him to marry Ruth himself? Boaz's plan offers ample scope for it to backfire. Boaz's tactics potentially reveal a degree of ambivalence in his approach to the entire matter. He has already signaled to Ruth that he may not be able to redeem her (Ruth 3:13); after all, he does not say unequivocally that he will marry her, only if *Peloni Almoni* is not prepared to redeem her, then he will. Many things may be holding Boaz back—such as the homosocial relationships he has built with his male reapers, Ruth's Moabite ethnicity, his apparent status as a confirmed bachelor, and/or the boundaries of Ruth and Naomi's relationship and how this situation may affect him and any marriage to Ruth. But if we trust Naomi's words to Ruth in Ruth 3:18 ("the man will not be still until the matter is finished today"), Boaz does not have the luxury of unpacking his own feelings before having to deal with settling the matter one way or another.[6] He is goaded into action, which may explain why he approaches the matter in this risky fashion.

In verse 4, Boaz presents the issue of the field to *Peloni Almoni.* Employing verbs of the root .ל.א.ג (*G'l*), "redeem," five times in his direct speech, Boaz stresses to *Peloni Almoni* that the field is part of the process of redemption. Of course, the field is also a property with economic value, which Boaz is dangling, carrot-like, in front of *Peloni Almoni.* But as soon as *Peloni Almoni* agrees to redeem the field, Boaz throws in the subject of marriage to Ruth; the field and Ruth come as a package.

Boaz's response in verse 5, however, is unclear and much discussed.[7] The questions it raises can be summarized as follows: Is the field the property of

Naomi alone or of both Naomi *and* Ruth? And which is the better reading
of this verse, the *qere* or the *ketiv*, which I elucidate subsequently? Whether
the property is Naomi's alone is not ultimately determinable here—though it
could potentially tie Boaz, Naomi, and Ruth more closely together should, as
eventually happens, Boaz redeem the field on behalf of both women. More
curious yet is the *qere ketiv*. Does Boaz suggest that marriage to Ruth (via
some form of levirate process) is a package deal, along with the purchase of
the field, as per the *qere*, which reads קָנִיתָ (*qānîtā*; "you will acquire"), or
rather does he state that whatever happens, he, Boaz, will acquire Ruth as a
wife, as per the *ketiv*, which reads קָנִיתִי (*qānt*; "I will acquire")? If the latter
reading is accepted, as supported by Linafelt (among others), then Boaz never
puts his relationship with Ruth at risk at all.[8]

Either way, the trap is sprung for *Peloni Almoni* if his sole motivation is
to redeem the field and enrich himself. *Peloni Almoni* clearly has not connected the question of redemption of the field to a levirate marriage to Ruth.
Should *Peloni Almoni* marry Ruth, then, according to Boaz, *Peloni Almoni*
is also required to produce an heir with her to take over her dead husband's
inheritance. If, instead, Boaz marries Ruth, then Boaz will produce the heir
who will take over the field in due course. Either way, *Peloni Almoni* is no
more than a caretaker for the field until an heir is produced; hence, realizing
this trap, *Peloni Almoni* declines to redeem the field on the basis that it will
put his own estate at risk (verse 6).

From a narrative standpoint, *Peloni Almoni* was never much more than a
device for raising a modicum of false jeopardy. Yet not only the question of
Boaz's motivations and intentions but also the overall purpose of this sub-
plot remain. The real question may be not "Why does Boaz enact this risky
strategy?" but "Why does the narrator interject the closer kinsman into the
narrative at all?" The story's plot does not require the additional complica-
tion of a closer redeemer and levirate marriage in order to find its resolution
in a satisfactory way. Ruth 4:1–10 could simply be deleted from the text and
replaced with a single verse testifying that Boaz took Ruth as his wife. Superficially, nothing about the plot would change at all. So why is this plot twist
part of the story? The answers may lie in the public display of bureaucracy
that follows in verses 7–10.

EXCURSUS ON LEVIRATE MARRIAGE (RUTH 4:7–10)

Much has been written about the subject of levirate marriage in the Book of
Ruth and its apparent conflation with redemption (from *G'l*).[9] The legal process of a levirate marriage is described in Deut. 25:5–10, where the text refers
to the case of two brothers, one of whom dies childless and leaves a widow.

The surviving brother is then required to "take" his brother's widow and produce a male heir, who will carry the name and receive the inheritance of the deceased man. If the surviving brother refuses to carry out this duty, then, in a ceremony known as *halizah*, the widow pulls off her brother-in-law's sandal, spits in his face, and makes a declaration in front of the elders who serve as witnesses.[10] The surviving brother is shamed by being known as בֵּית חֲלוּץ הַנָּעַל (*bêt ḥălûṣ hannā'al*), "the house of the one without a sandal."

In Ruth 4:7–10, the narrator appears superficially to describe the ceremony of *halizah*. A sandal is removed, and a declaration is made in front of the elders. But there are crucial differences. Ruth is not involved at all. *Peloni Almoni* is the one who takes off his own sandal while speaking to Boaz. Boaz is the one who makes a declaration, which includes not merely marriage to Ruth but also the acquisition of Naomi's field. No one spits in anyone's face. *Peloni Almoni* is not shamed in any fashion, and no appellation is attached to him. Moreover, in verse 7, the narrator seeks to justify what is about to happen by setting the scene with an explanation of how things were done in Israel in earlier times—again, a description that does not conform to Deut. 25:5–10, nor to any other text (legal or narrative) in the Hebrew Bible.

Indeed, apart from Deut. 25, the only other biblical passage that appears to describe levirate marriage is Gen. 38 (a chapter also alluded to later). Gen. 38 contains the story of Jacob's son, Judah, and Tamar, another non-Israelite woman who must exercise resourcefulness and find a creative way to produce a male heir following the death of her Israelite husband. Following one unsuccessful levirate marriage, Judah, Tamar's father-in-law, refrains from giving his remaining son in levirate marriage. Consequently, Tamar disguises herself as a sex worker and seduces Judah, which results in the birth of male twins, Perez and Zerah.

The intertextual allusion to Tamar is widely employed to shore up support for the idea that what is happening in the Book of Ruth is also some form of levirate marriage.[11] Both Ruth and Tamar are foreign women. Both Tamar and Ruth must employ proactive seduction in order to bear heirs. Both Perez and Obed (the latter being the offspring of Ruth and Boaz's union) are part of the same genealogy cited in Ruth 4:18–22. Yet both stories deviate considerably from the laws of levirate marriage described in Deut. 25. The intertextual allusions between the stories are undoubtedly important, but not because either story makes a compelling case for the real-life practices of levirate marriage. Rather, both cases clearly raise questions about why any recourse to levirate marriage is necessary at all.

Few commentators have addressed this matter directly. An exception is Tamara Cohn Eskenazi, who explicitly asks, "Why does he go about it [marriage to Ruth] in the complicated, confusing manner described in the book?"[12] By way of explanation, Eskenazi points to Deut. 23:4—the prohibition against the admission of Moabites into the Israelite community. Boaz knows that his proposed marriage to Ruth, the Moabitess, falls outside of the norms of Israelite society and, therefore, seeks to construct a publicly witnessed and sanctioned ceremony that will confer approval on his marriage. Employing *both* the language of redemption *and* recognizable parts of levirate marriage/*halizah*, even while not conforming to every part of the actual Deuteronomic rules of levirate marriage, the narrator portrays Boaz as someone who "shrewdly builds community support for his intentions by expanding the communally sanctioned tradition of the redeeming kinsman."[13] In order to ensure both that his marriage to a forbidden Moabite is viewed by the community as socially acceptable and that any offspring resulting from this union would be deemed legitimate, Boaz draws on recognizable legal norms to create the illusion of legality and respectability.

Eskenazi's reading is compelling, but it does not take into account the question of the field. Why does Boaz raise the issue of the field at all? It has nothing to do with Ruth's ethnic identity or the prohibitions in Deut. 23. If Boaz's only concern is around the acceptance of his marriage to a Moabitess, then why bring up the matter of the field? An element of these verses may be about smoothing over the problems presented by the prohibition against marriage to Moabites, but this element is only one part of the conundrum. In linking the redemption of the field to marriage to Ruth, Boaz is tying himself not only to Ruth but also to Naomi.

From the perspective of a polyamorous hermeneutic, Boaz ensures that *both* women are provided for through him. He is bonding all three of them together, albeit by different means in the case of each woman. Moreover, Boaz expresses regard for each woman in a different way, appropriate to her needs. In the case of Ruth, who has already directly approached Boaz about marriage, Boaz creates a means to enable a publicly sanctioned union between the two of them. In the case of Naomi, with whom the text never reveals direct contact, Boaz nevertheless finds a creative way to express his regard for her by ensuring that her well-being and prosperity are secured through the redemption of her field. Boaz is sensitive to the different needs of both Ruth and Naomi, engaging in a solution for each of them that fits within the limitations and bounds of ancient Israelite society. Although, given the patriarchal structures within which Boaz is acting, he appears to be the one with all of the power, his solution in wielding this power grants both Ruth and Naomi what they need. Moreover, Boaz plays up to the expected power dynamics within his society, outwardly treating the transfer of Ruth the same way he treats the transfer of the field. Both superficially appear as transactions decided by men without the consent of the women involved. But Boaz is knowingly and actively enacting Ruth's will, as expressed to him in Chapter 3, and the reader knows that he is also enacting the will of Naomi, who instructed Ruth and created the space for a marriage in the first place. From this perspective, all three of them are consenting, in however a "fuzzy, messy, or icky" fashion, to the marriage of Boaz and Ruth, which also includes and provides for Naomi.[14]

The matter of the redemption of the field is more oblique but equally important. The reader cannot plausibly assume that Naomi would actively wish for the field to remain unredeemed, so Boaz's actions can be assumed to express an altruistic desire for Naomi's well-being—or, at the very least, an acceptance of his moral and ethical responsibilities toward her. Either way, Boaz is presented as being concerned about Naomi's welfare. Without the matter of the field being part of his negotiations with *Peloni Almoni*, Boaz's concern for Naomi would never have been made explicit. And without the muddling up of the matter with the pseudo-legality of levirate marriage/*halizah*, Boaz's concern for Naomi might too easily have been exposed as a major component of his plan. If Boaz's long-term strategy is to build a polyamorous family, both redemption and levirate marriage are necessary parts of his ingenious reimagining of known legal norms to create a socially acceptable, outward-facing structure of legality for this non-normative (or alternative) family.[15]

Indeed, through the clever use of both levirate marriage and redemption of the field, the text makes clear what each of the three parties brings to the relationship: Boaz brings wealth, status, and at least the illusion of the cover of heteropatriarchal normativity. Ruth brings the possibility of her fertility. Naomi brings property in the form of the field.[16] Not only are Naomi and Ruth linked through their long-standing relationship with each other going back at least ten years to their time in Moab, but Naomi and Boaz are also linked through their long-standing kinship relationship, and with the added redemption of property, and now Ruth and Boaz will be linked through the formal, legal ties of marriage. This three-way bond connects them inextricably; surely the recipe for a stable, closed, mutual, polyamorous relationship that will enable them to all be the progenitors of the next generation, Obed.

THE BLESSINGS (RUTH 4:11–12)

Having ensured that the elders serve as witnesses (verse 9), Boaz resolves the entire situation (verse 10). In verse 11, all of the people, both the elders and everyone at the gates, exclaim blessings upon Boaz and "the woman coming into your [Boaz's] house." Noteworthy here is that they do not explicitly name Ruth, though surely she is the one intended by "the woman." Nevertheless, in describing only "the woman coming into your house," on the one hand, the words leave open the possibility that either Ruth or Naomi is meant and, on the other, draw attention to the differences between the two. Hence,

Naomi (presumably) is not coming into Boaz's house; rather, he acquires her house. Ruth comes as part of that acquisition. The house of Naomi (i.e., all that belonged to her husband and sons) appears to be subsumed into the house of Boaz—far more than merely the transfer of a field. The question left unaddressed is where Naomi fits into that acquisition. Is Naomi, too, obliquely a "woman who is coming into your house"?

The blessings of verses 11–12 offer two key intertextual allusions: the first is to Rachel and Leah, as the women who built the family of Israel, and the second is to Judah and Tamar (as discussed previously), as the progenitors of the genealogical line to which Boaz belongs. In particular, this first blessing, regarding Rachel and Leah, alludes to *two* named women, both wives of Jacob, not one. Can Ruth truly be understood as the sole recipient of this two-fold blessing, or, again, does citing two women here obliquely allude to *both* Ruth *and* Naomi, despite the singular construction of "the woman coming into your house"?

Ilana Pardes has written extensively on the ways in which Ruth and Naomi's relationship heals the rifts in biblical female relationships that exist (though do not originate) in Rachel and Leah's fractious sister-wives relationship.[17] Where Rachel and Leah compete with each other not only for Jacob's affection but also, and more important, in this context, for how many children (particularly sons) they can provide him with, Ruth and Naomi work together to ensure the continuation of the familial line that is linked back to Judah, the son of Jacob and Leah. Leah is compelled to apply her greater fertility to compete with her sister Rachel for Jacob's love and attachment.[18] By contrast, Naomi has already acknowledged her own lack of fertility. Instead, she devises a plan and instructs Ruth to ensure that Ruth, who is theoretically fertile (remembering that she has not had any children despite ten years of marriage), can produce an heir with Boaz.[19] Where Naomi and Ruth work together, Rachel and Leah vie against each other. Pardes sees the Book of Ruth as "an intriguing rewriting of Genesis."[20] Moreover, she writes,

> The representation of triangular dynamics in this text [the Book of Ruth] is indeed strikingly unconventional . . . the representation of the ties of Naomi-Ruth-Boaz reveals a significant break from the traditional scene where two women compete for the same man. We find here . . . the resurgence of the preoedipal triangular structure in which the privileged term is not the all-powerful father, but an adored mother. What the Book of Ruth thus completes in its rewriting of Genesis is the possible impact of the preoedipal phase on women's relations.[21]

But even though Pardes comes very close to imagining a properly triadic relationship between Naomi, Ruth, and Boaz, she stops short of saying so.[22]

Instead, Pardes centers Naomi as the key figure in the story, the "adored mother," as opposed to the more normative "all-powerful father" (as Jacob is in the context of the Leah and Rachel narrative). In shifting the focus, Pardes sees the Naomi-Ruth relationship as a sort of healing of the Rachel–Leah relationship.

But I would go further than Pardes. Rachel and Leah, married to Jacob, present the archetypal example of a dysfunctional patriarchal polygamous family. The primary focus is on the patriarch and his progeny, which is to the detriment of his wives' emotional well-being.[23] Leah and Rachel are incapable of forming an emotionally sustaining bond with each other. The closest they come to mutual support is a brief moment of *détente* in Gen. 30:14–15, where, in return for aphrodisiac mandrakes found by Leah's son Reuben, Rachel allows her sister a night with Jacob—during which Leah conceives, which reignites the sisters' competition. Ultimately, this rare moment of cooperation between the sister-wives is of greatest benefit to Jacob, who is rewarded with yet another son. Leah and Rachel, however, remain emotionally detached from each other. Neither Rachel nor Leah is capable of expressing any degree of compersion for the other.

Ruth and Naomi stand in sharp relief to Rachel and Leah. Ruth and Naomi are not sisters, who are inescapably bound to each other, but rather women who have made the active choice to remain together. They do not compete with each other for the love and attention of Boaz. Rather, in an expression of compersion, Naomi has actively expressed her aim of seeking rest for Ruth through marriage to Boaz. Though Boaz serves as the glue that ties the three of them together, he does so through a genuine attempt to meet the needs of both women and without disrupting Ruth and Naomi's existing relationship. Through marriage, redemption, and acts of *hesed*, Ruth, Naomi, and Boaz become the exemplars of the best of what might have been possible during the biblical period: an emotionally literate polyamorous family—an example of polyamorous polygamy in which all three members build up one another.

The second part of the blessing in verse 12 draws parallels with the story of Judah and Tamar, normally understood as an allusion to levirate marriage, as discussed previously. This part of the blessing also makes explicit that the people, both the elders and everyone else sitting at the gates, will regard any offspring from Boaz's marriage to Ruth as a legitimate Israelite heir. They cite specifically the house of Perez, thereby signposting the genealogy that begins with Perez that will conclude the book. Because this genealogy concludes ten generations later with the birth of David, establishing the legitimacy of the progeny of this polyamorous polygamous family is crucial.

NAOMI ASCENDANT OR A TRIADIC
HAPPILY EVER AFTER? (RUTH 4:13–17)

וַיִּקַּח בֹּעַז אֶת־רוּת וַתְּהִי־לוֹ לְאִשָּׁה וַיָּבֹא אֵלֶיהָ וַיִּתֵּן יְהוָה לָהּ הֵרָיוֹן וַתֵּלֶד בֵּן:

13 Boaz took Ruth. She was a wife to him. He came to her. The Eternal One
gave to her pregnancy. She gave birth to a son.

Once the blessings have been bestowed, the narrative reverts to the now-
familiar contraction of time. Within the span of a single verse (verse 13),
Boaz marries Ruth; she becomes his wife; he goes to her; she conceives; and,
finally, she bears a son. In the best-case scenario, Boaz and Ruth are married
the same day, have sexual intercourse that evening, and she becomes pregnant on the first try, followed by a normal gestation period of forty weeks,
labor, and birth.[24] Again, the narrator describes nothing to the reader of what
happens during this passage of time. Boaz marries Ruth, but what happens
to Naomi? Where does she live? Is Ruth fulfilling her vow in Ruth 1:16 to
lodge wherever Naomi lodges? If so, logically, we must infer that Naomi has
moved in with the happy couple. How did the three of them live together?
Did Naomi and Ruth fall back on well-established patterns of maintaining a
home together? How did Naomi react to Ruth's pregnancy? These questions
and many more arise, much as did the questions about day-to-day life in the
ten years that Ruth, Naomi, and Orpah lived together. The lacuna must be
noted here as well, for it tells us much about the priorities of the storyteller,
as opposed to the reader. Where the narrator may be in a hurry to give the
reader the "action highlights," as readers, we may well be interested in imag-
ing the details.

The text states וַיִּקַּח בֹּעַז אֶת־רוּת (*wayyiqqaḥ bōʿaz ʾet-rût*), "Boaz took Ruth,"
employing a common biblical verb denoting marriage. The use of ל.ק.ח.
stands in contradistinction to the use of נ.שׂ.א. in Ruth 1:4. If the use of נ.שׂ.א.
connotes a nonconsensual rape-marriage (as postulated by Gafney), then
perhaps the conscious use of a different root here, ל.ק.ח., could indicate the
consensual nature of Ruth and Boaz's union.[25]

Moreover, the narrator makes a point of stating that not only does Boaz
"take" Ruth, but also וַתְּהִי־לוֹ לְאִשָּׁה (*wattəhî-lô ləʾiššāh*), "and she became his
wife." This phraseology could provide another important clue as to Boaz's
feelings toward Ruth. The construction may suggest an intertextual allusion
to the similarly phrased marital union of Isaac and Rebekah in Gen. 24:67
וַיִּקַּח אֶת־רִבְקָה וַתְּהִי־לוֹ לְאִשָּׁה, "and he took Rebekah and she became his wife."[26]
Here the union is followed by וַיֶּאֱהָבֶהָ (*wayyeʾĕhābehā*), "and he loved her."
Additionally, Gen. 24:57 suggests that Rebekah actively consented to her
marriage to Isaac, albeit in the limited fashion available to her.[27] Might the

narrator be hinting at the same for Ruth and Boaz—that Boaz loved Ruth and that, in whatever limited fashion was available to her, she consented to their marriage?

Finally, Ruth is blessed with a pregnancy. The phrase וַיִּתֵּן יְהֹוָה לָהּ הֵרָיוֹן (*wayyittēn 'ădōnāi lāh hērāyôn*), "The Eternal One gave her pregnancy," is unique to the Book of Ruth. Although the Hebrew Bible contains many examples of divinely approved pregnancies among women who have previously been barren, Ruth was never described as barren.[28] Moreover, God is not described elsewhere as granting a pregnancy in precisely this language.[29] Why does God intervene here in this way? Why does sexual intercourse between Boaz and Ruth not suffice to produce a child?

Interestingly in this context, according to Ruth Rabbah 7:7, "Rabbi Berekhya said: Thus expounded two world greats, Rabbi Eliezer and Rabbi Yehoshua: Boaz did his and Ruth did hers and Naomi did hers. The Holy Blessed One said: 'Moreover, I will do mine.'"[30] Even the rabbis appear to understand that the story of Ruth rests not on two actors but on three, all of whom must work together for the common good. If the three central characters can work together to the benefit of all, then God, too, must do God's part. The birth of this son, Obed, is not merely the result of Boaz and Ruth's sexual union but also the effective engagement of all three of them to bring about God's desire to act. Three, not the usual two, is the magic number that ensures God's commitment to this family.[31]

Following the divine intervention in the birth of Obed, verse 14 begins with the women of Bethlehem speaking to Naomi.[32] They bless God, who has not withheld a redeemer from Naomi, and ask for "his" name to be exclaimed in Israel. Although the identity of the redeemer is not immediately clear in this verse, verse 15 clarifies that the redeemer is the child. Additionally, precisely *whose* identity is to be exclaimed in Israel (i.e., the redeemer's or God's) is also somewhat obscure.[33] Why do the women not identify the redeemer as Boaz, who has redeemed Naomi's field and married her daughter-in-law, procuring an heir, and who has in every legal sense acted as a redeemer? Perhaps they don't, because identifying Boaz as the redeemer would grant him disproportionate importance in the Boaz-Ruth-Naomi triad and leave that relationship imbalanced.

Instead, they identify Obed as the one to unify the triadic relationship. Obed is Naomi's redeemer, who, according to the women, will revive her soul and sustain her in her old age. But the women also acknowledge that he is the product of her daughter-in-law's womb, the woman who loves Naomi and is better to her than seven sons. Naomi does not have a redeemer without Ruth. Ruth, though neither addressed directly nor mentioned by name, is essential to Naomi. They are intimately bound together.

Indeed, verse 15 is the only one in the Hebrew Bible to use the root א.ה.ב. (*'hb*), "love," in the context of two women.[34] The force of that love is much

debated among commentators. The use of אֲהֵבַתֶךְ (*'ăhēbatek*) has been central
to contemporary readings of Ruth and Naomi as lesbians, for example, in
contradistinction to traditional readings of this term.[35] In Biblical Hebrew,
א.ה.ב. can be used to denote many types of love (e.g., friendship, loyalty,
affection, romantic, sexual, and divine)—hence the need to determine from
context the type of love intended.[36] What becomes important in verse 15 is
not so much the exact nature of the love but rather the fact that it is mentioned
at all. The women of Bethlehem reflect something key back to Naomi—that
Ruth loves her and, therefore, Ruth is better than seven sons. In a polyamorous relationship, the type of love expressed by members of the group may
fluctuate as they express and explore their own gender identities, sexual
orientations, and relations to each member of the union within the bounds
of their relationship. That reality fits well with the ambiguity here about
what precise type of love the women of Bethlehem see reflected in Ruth and
Naomi's relationship. Naomi had formerly been despondent about the lack
of a relationship to sustain her (Ruth 1:19); now the women of Bethlehem
are able to draw her attention to her unique relationship with Ruth and to its
source of love and sustenance.

But, as the women of Bethlehem also point out, Naomi's welfare comes
by way of the redemption provided by the son of Boaz and Ruth. Verse
16 makes this point even more explicit when Naomi takes the child—וַתִּקַּח
(*wattiqqah*)—from the same root ל.ק.ח. used in verse 13 for Boaz's marriage
to Ruth. "Take" in English, as in Biblical Hebrew, can be a rather inelegant
word, signifying too often the objectification of whatever (or more point-
edly, as in this case, whoever) is being taken. But perhaps in both these
usages, a better way of understanding the root might be "to take in"—that
is, to make someone formally part of one's family. In this sense, Naomi
publicly and formally makes Obed part of her family, much as Boaz has
done with Ruth.

Similarly, Boaz "went to" Ruth, consummating their marriage through a
physical, bodily act, and Naomi physically enacts the inclusion of the child
into her family by putting him on her breast. She thereby becomes his foster
mother. Although inverted, again the verse is constructed similarly to verse
13 (see figure 9.1). Boaz takes Ruth; she becomes his wife; he has sexual
intercourse with her. Naomi takes the child; she breastfeeds him (either literally or symbolically); and she becomes his foster mother. Structurally, both
verses describe a process of incorporation into the family.

Viewed in this light, two families appear superficially to be emerging—
Ruth and Boaz, Naomi and Obed. But the women of Bethlehem have also
clearly drawn out the familial relationship between Naomi and Ruth. Ruth
is part of both of these families, a heteropatriarchal one with Boaz and a
homomatriarchal one with Naomi. But just like *hesed* has bound Boaz, Ruth,
and Naomi together, so, too, will Obed. He is biologically the child of Ruth

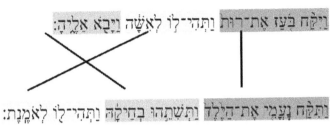

Figure 9.1 **Structural Comparison of Ruth 4:13 and 16.** *Source*: Image created by the author.

and Boaz and is ceremonially incorporated into the family of Naomi. Effectively, Obed is "birthed" twice—once physically by Ruth and once ritually by Naomi. *Hesed* and the birth of a male heir draw these potential tensions between different types of dyadic relationships toward the possibility of a polyamorous, triadic resolution.

The final piece in this puzzle is in verse 17. Here the women, now named explicitly as neighbors, declare openly that "a son is born to Naomi," concluding the ritual that she has enacted in verse 16. The women of her neighborhood recognize that Obed is part of Naomi's family as well as the reverse—that Naomi is part of Obed's family.[37] Finally, the women name him עוֹבֵד (*'ōḇēḏ*), Obed, from the root ע.ב.ד., which broadly means "to work, labor, serve, or worship."[38] The name may suggest that Obed is subservient to Naomi and her family, but it equally may portray him as the end product of the work of her relationships. He is the child for whom she, Ruth, and Boaz have had to toil and who would not exist without the efforts of all three.

THE GENEALOGY (RUTH 4:18–22)

The book ends with the genealogy of David, starting ten generations earlier with Perez. Finally, in this genealogy, Obed is named as the son of Boaz, not Naomi or, indeed, Ruth.[39] Verse 21 explicitly states that "Boaz begat Obed." This genealogy redirects the reader away from the story of Ruth, Naomi, and Boaz and back to the decidedly terse, clear, and unequivocal patriarchal family line that will produce David. Whatever other stories the Book of Ruth has been telling—lesbian, homosocial, and polyamorous ones—ultimately, these have been reincorporated into the (apparently) normative, patriarchal, and overarching historical narrative at the core of the Hebrew Bible. The genealogy acts almost like a "beard," attempting to conceal the sexual complexities of the story and instead redirecting the reader's attention to King David of Israel and to the hyper-patriarchal masculinity of kingship.

The genealogy is not incidental or tacked on; it is fundamental in misdirecting the reader away from the radical stories within the text.

NOTES

1. *Peloni Almoni*, "so and so," is hardly a character at all. His name makes it clear that he is really just a plot device, rather than a meaningful threat to Boaz.

2. The significant passage relating to female inheritance in the Hebrew Bible is Num. 36:1–12, which discusses the case of the daughters of Zelophehad, but this passage discusses only the circumstances under which a daughter may inherit. For more information about women's inheritance in the Hebrew Bible, see Judith Hauptman, *Rereading the Rabbis: A Woman's Voice* (Boulder, CO: Westview Press, 1998), 177–79.

3. Cf. Eskenazi and Frymer-Kensky, *The JPS Bible Commentary: Ruth*, 73; Schipper, *The Anchor Yale Bible: Ruth*, 173.

4. Even Schipper mentions this fact only in a throwaway comment: "Naomi and Boaz seem to have knowledge of each other's actions even though they never appear in the same scene anywhere in the book" (Schipper, *The Anchor Yale Bible: Ruth*, 173). Yet Schipper never questions why this might be the case.

5. Schipper comments, "The fact that no one raises any objections to the redemption of this portion of the field may imply that Boaz represents Naomi's intentions accurately . . . it is also possible that Boaz's claim about the sale shows that he has the capacity to lie or be manipulative" (Schipper, *The Anchor Yale Bible: Ruth*, 173). What is implicit here, though Schipper does not spell it out, is that Naomi's intentions are known—to Boaz and/or the elders who are serving as witnesses. That could only be the case if Naomi has communicated to Boaz and/ or the elders to make her intentions known. Again, the simplest explanation is that Naomi has spoken with Boaz, though this conversation was not reported by the narrator.

6. How does Naomi know that Boaz will not rest until he has settled the matter that same day? Perhaps she is merely expressing what she assumes will be the case. Alternatively, her conviction here suggests that she knows Boaz better than the narrator lets on, which points obliquely, again, to the possibility of conversation and/or interaction between Boaz and Naomi that is not recorded in the text.

7. For example, Schipper, *The Anchor Yale Bible: Ruth*, 165–67.

8. Linafelt, *Berit Olam*, 68. However, Linafelt's interpretation fails to take into account Ruth 3:12–13. If Boaz always intends to marry Ruth, then why doesn't he just explain to her that he has to sort out the problem of the field first?

9. The word "levirate" is derived from the Latin word *levir*, for husband's brother.

   For a summary of the distinctions between redemption and levirate marriage and how they function together in Ruth, see Steffan Mathias, *Paternity, Progeny, and Perpetuation: Creating Lives After Death in the Hebrew Bible* (London: T&T Clark, 2020), 214–25.

10. *Halizah* stems from the Hebrew root ח.ל.צ., meaning "loosen, take off, be taken off," *DCH Vol III* ט-ז, 239. See its use in Deut. 25:9: וְחָלְצָה נַעֲלוֹ מֵעַל רַגְלוֹ (*Wəhāləṣāh naʿălô mēʿal raglô*), "and his sandal is taken off his foot." The root is used again, as quoted, in Deut. 25:10.

11. For more information on levirate marriage, see Mathias, *Paternity, Progeny, and Perpetuation*, 192–222, as well as Dvora E. Weisberg, "The Widow of Our Discontent: Levirate Marriage in the Bible and Ancient Israel," *Journal for the Study of the Old Testament* 28 (2004): 403–29, and Eryl W. Davies, "Inheritance Rights and the Hebrew Levirate Marriage," *Vetus Testamentum* 31 (1981): 138–44, 257–68. Both articles, particularly part 2 (257–68) of Davies, deal specifically with both the story of Tamar and the story of Ruth.

12. Eskenazi and Frymer-Kensky, *The JPS Bible Commentary: Ruth*, xxxiii.

13. Eskenazi and Frymer-Kensky, *The JPS Bible Commentary: Ruth*, xxxiii.

14. Cf. Levine, "Biblical Women's Marital Rights," 126–28. For Naomi, being a co-wife would have been a safer position in society than remaining as a widow on her own. See also Mona West, "Ruth," in *The Queer Bible Commentary*, edited by Deryn Guest, Robert E. Goss, Mona West, and Thomas Bohache (London: SCM Press, 2006), 193:

> All of these actions speak to Naomi, Ruth, and Boaz's decision to create their own family and define their own understanding of kinship and responsibility to one another within the context of the inheritance and kinship laws of ancient Israel. These actions are similar to the ways in which queer people of today create families: a bisexual man and two lesbians live together with their biological child; a gay man is a sperm donor for a lesbian couple and takes part in the parenting their child; three gay men live together as lovers and family for twenty years; a lesbian mother and her lover live two doors down from her lesbian daughter and her lover.

15. Additional proof of this plan can also be seen in the lack of shaming of *Peloni Almoni*. The purpose of shaming in the *halizah* ritual is likely to make an example of men who fail to do their duty in levirate marriage. But in this circumstance, Boaz does not want to make an example of *Peloni Almoni* at all. He wants to draw attention away from the idea that *Peloni Almoni* should have acted as redeemer/*levir* and, instead, signal that nothing unusual is happening here that anyone needs to worry about. Boaz is just being a decent man and solving a small problem around a field and an otherwise unmarriageable woman.

Cf. Berquist, "Role Differentiation in the Book of Ruth," 33–34:

> Surprisingly, Boaz volunteers for the role of Ruth's husband (4.5, 10). This is a permanent legal role; Boaz, the husband, must provide for Ruth and Naomi for the rest of their lives, unless divorce should sever the relationship. Were Boaz the only redeemer, then the one-time transfer of funds would have continued the marginal existence and social isolation of Naomi and Ruth. However, the new role of husband creates a long-term relationship between Boaz and the women that grants them society's greatest guarantees of economic and social security.

16. Of course, they each bring other personal qualities to their relationship as well, but in terms of *tachlis*, the practical matters that are externally visible, these are the things they bring.

17. Ilana Pardes, "The Book of Ruth: Idyllic Revisionism," in *Countertraditions in the Bible: A Feminist Approach* (Cambridge, MA: Harvard University Press, 1992), 98–117.

18. Gen. 30:31–35; in particular, note the language of hatred (verses 31 and 33), love (verse 32), and attachment (verse 34).

19. Cf. Ruth Rabbah 7:14, which states that on the day that Boaz married Ruth, "Rabbi Simon ben Lakish said that she [Ruth] didn't have a womb, but the Holiness, Be God Blessed, carved a womb for her."

20. Pardes, "The Book of Ruth," 102.

21. Pardes, "The Book of Ruth," 103.

22. Exum also refers to the Ruth-Naomi-Boaz relationship as a triangle: Exum, *Plotted, Shot, and Painted: Cultural Representations of Biblical Women*, 168.

23. And often the children as well, as is typified by the dysfunctionality of the relationships between Jacob's sons and their fratricidal behaviour.

24. This succession of events is effectively what is imagined by the tenth-century midrashic collection, Ruth Zutta, where it recounts that Boaz died on his wedding night (presumably postcoitus): Ruth Zutta 4:13.

25. Gafney, "Mother Knows Best," 29.

However, Gen. 34:2, in which Shechem "takes" Dinah, followed by sleeping with her and humiliating her, suggests that ל.ק.ח. could also involve forced, not consensual, sex.

26. The phrase וַתְּהִי־לוֹ לְאִשָּׁה also appears in 1 Sam. 25:42 (David and Abigail) and 2 Sam. 11:27 (David and Bathsheba). 1 Sam. 25:43 reads: וְאֶת־אֲחִינֹעַם לָקַח דָּוִד מִיִּזְרְעֶאל וַתִּהְיֶיןָ, גַּם־שְׁתֵּיהֶן לוֹ לְנָשִׁים:, "And David took Ahinoam from Jezreel and the two of them also became his wives." This verse is the only other example of the text employing both "taking" and "she/they became his wife/wives," though the possible meaning of this intertextual allusion is less clear.

27. Rebekah's brother, Laban, and her father, Bethuel, had already promised Rebekah in marriage (Gen. 24:50); nevertheless, her brother and mother ask for her consent to depart with Abraham's servant in order to marry Isaac.

28. Eskenazi and Frymer-Kensky, *The JPS Bible Commentary: Ruth*, 87–88. For other examples of divinely approved pregnancies, see Gen. 4:1 (Eve), 21:2 (Sarah), 25:21 (Rebekah), and 29:32–33 (Rachel); Judg. 13:3 (Samson's mother); and 1 Sam. 1:20 (Hannah).

29. Cf. the story of Hannah. In 1 Sam. 1:6, Hannah's rival and co-wife taunts her, saying that "the Eternal One closed her womb." Later, after Hannah prays, 1 Sam. 1:19 states, "the Eternal One remembered her," and in the next verse she conceives. Also, cf. Sarah, Gen. 21:1: "The Eternal One paid attention to Sarah as promised."

30. אָמַר רַבִּי בֶּרֶכְיָה, כָּךְ דָּרְשׁוּ שְׁנֵי גְדוֹלֵי עוֹלָם, רַבִּי אֱלִיעֶזֶר וְרַבִּי יְהוֹשֻׁעַ, רַבִּי אֱלִיעֶזֶר אוֹמֵר בֹּעַז עָשָׂה אֶת שֶׁלּוֹ, וְרוּת עָשְׂתָה אֶת שֶׁלָּהּ, וְנָעֳמִי עָשְׂתָה אֶת שֶׁלָּהּ, אָמַר הַקָּדוֹשׁ בָּרוּךְ הוּא, אַף אֲנִי אֶעֱשֶׂה אֶת שֶׁלִּי.

31. Although I would not suggest that the rabbis were actively granting their "seal of approval" to a polyamorous union, perhaps this midrash could serve as a theological basis for the implication of divine approval.

32. Perhaps even the same women who did not recognize Naomi on her return from Moab in Ruth 1:19.

33. Cf. Schipper, *The Anchor Yale Bible: Ruth*, 179.

34. Indeed, the root is employed only once, when a woman loves a man. In 1 Sam. 18:20, Michal is described as loving David, the descendant of this Ruth-Naomi-Boaz relationship.

35. For a beautiful but more subtle rendering of this idea, see the contemporary Israeli midrash from *Dirshuni II*, Book of Ruth III 15: ומניין היה להן לשכנות לקרוא לנולד על שם נעמי ולא על שם מחלון, והלוא הכתוב אומר 'כי ישבו אחים יחדו ומת אחד מהם ובן אין לו...' והיה הבכור אשר תלד יקום על שם אחיו המת' (דברים כה, ו)?אלא שראו אהבת רות לנעמי כאהבת אלקנה לחנה, וקראו: 'כי כלתך אשר אהבתך ילדתו אשר היא טובה לך משבעה בנים (רות ד, טו). This midrash asks why Obed is named as the son of Naomi and not, as the levirate process would require, as the son of Mahlon. The answer given is that because Ruth loved Naomi in the same way that Elkanah loved Hannah, suggesting a parity of love between a same-sex and an opposite-sex couple.

36. For a broad analysis of the range of meanings of 'hb, see Gerhard Wallis, "אָהַב," in *The Theological Dictionary of the Old Testament Vol I* אב-זדד (abh-badhadh), edited by G. Johannes Botterwick and Helmer Ringgen (Grand Rapids, MI: William B. Eerdmans, 1977), 99–118. See also Ellen van Wolde, "Sentiments as Culturally Constructed Emotions: Anger and Love in the Hebrew Bible," *Biblical Interpretation* 16 (2008): 1–24, particularly 18–22. Van Wolde looks specifically at the instances in which 'hb is used between a man and a woman in the Hebrew Bible (and excludes all instances of its use in Song of Songs). She does not discuss the use of 'hb in Ruth 4:15. Also, Brenner, *I Am . . .*, 8–30.

37. Verse 16 reads וַתְּהִי־לוֹ לְאֹמֶנֶת, "she was to him a foster mother"; the construction implies that she belonged to him in the same way that וַתְּהִי־לוֹ לְאִשָּׁה ("she was to him a wife") in verse 13 implies that she belonged to Boaz.

38. *DCH Vol VI* פ-ס, 209–15.

39. Ruth is named explicitly as the mother of Obed in Matt. 1:5 in his genealogy of Jesus. This genealogy mentions a few women (notably Tamar as the mother of Perez), but it does not as a matter of course mention mothers.

Chapter 10

The Book of Ruth

A Targum with Annotations (2024): Another Way of Telling the Story

This Targum will make explicit what has up to now been only hinted at in the text. Indeed, if we think of the whole of the Book of Ruth as a sort of public transcript, then this targumic version allows the hidden transcripts to emerge and erupt into the open. The indications of queerness and polyamory—as hinted at throughout the Book of Ruth, which I have highlighted throughout my commentary—can now be part of a new rendition of the text.

Although I have provided a very brief introduction to Targum in my introduction, I will say few words about Targum here for readers unfamiliar with the genre. A Targum is not only a translation in the sense of being a literal rendering of the Hebrew of the text into Aramaic, though in some instances it is certainly that. Undoubtedly some Targumim (notably, for example, Targum Onkelos) tend to be a more literal rendering of the Hebrew; other Targumim (such as Neofiti or Pseudo-Jonathan) contain rather more interpolated material. While Targum is often discussed as having sections of literal "translation" and sections of interpolated "interpretations," I prefer Simon Lasair's terminology, in which he distinguishes between "*one-to-one interlinguistic rendering* and *narrative expansion*" in Targumic texts.[1] I see my own Targum very much in the vein of "narrative expansion."

By way of example, here is Ruth 1:1:

> It happened during the days that the judges judged and there was a famine in the land, a man from Bethlehem in Judah went to live in the fields of Moab where there was at that time plenty: he, his wife, and two sons.

And here is the (English translation) of the same verse from the Targum to Ruth:

It came to pass in the days of the Judge of Judges that there was a great famine in the Land of Israel. Ten great famines were decreed by Heaven to be upon the earth, from the day on which the world was created until the coming of the King-Messiah, to admonish therewith the inhabitants of the earth. The first famine was in the days of Adam. The second famine was in the days of Lemech. The third was in the days of Abraham. The fourth famine was in the days of Isaac. The fifth famine was in the days of Jacob. The sixth famine was in the days of Boaz, who is known as Ivzan the Pious of Beth Lehem of Judah. The seventh famine was in the days of David, the king of Israel. The eighth famine was in the days of Elijah the prophet. The ninth famine was in the days of Elisha at Samaria. The tenth famine is due to come, not a famine of bread nor a thirst for water, but to hear the word of prophecy from the Lord. And when there was this great famine in the Land of Israel, a nobleman went forth out to Beth Lehem of Judah and went to dwell in the field of Moab, he and his wife and his two sons.[2]

Clearly this rendition is not a "one-to-one interlinguistic rendering," but rather far more of a "narrative expansion." Other verses, however, are much closer to a literal rendering than this one (e.g., Targum to Ruth 1:7).[3] This tension between a literal translation and narrative expansion will be a prominent feature of my own Targum. In doing so, my hope is that my Targum will have the feel of a classical Targum while expanding the narrative in a contemporary fashion.

Additionally, the endnotes to my Targum are, broadly, annotations. Annotations are a standard feature of the ways Jewish communities have studied our texts for millennia. For example, *Mikra'ot Gedolot* (also known as a rabbinic Bible) was the standard text for Jewish study of the Hebrew Bible for many centuries. Each page contains a small section of the text of the Hebrew Bible surrounded by the Targumim to the passage and numerous medieval Jewish commentaries. The aim of the annotations to my own Targum is to provide the reader with greater insight into my own thinking behind the production of this work.

A final note about the rubrics in this Targum: The literal "translation" is in the regular font.[4] Interpolations are in *italics*, as is the standard convention in English translations of the classical Targumim. The passages enclosed in { } are from interpolations in the (Aramaic) Targum to Ruth. Square brackets [] indicate insertions for sake of clarity in English but are not interpolations.

TARGUM RABBI DEBORAH TO RUTH[5]

Chapter 1

1. It happened during the days that the judges judged *that every person did what was good in their own eyes*[6] and there was a famine in the land

and there was none to decide between who would eat and who would go hungry;[7] *thus*, a man from Bethlehem in Judah went to live in the fields of Moab where there was at that time plenty: he, his wife, and two sons.

2. The name of the man was Elimelech and his wife's name, Naomi, and his two sons' names Mahlon and Chilion, Ephramites from Bethlehem in Judah. They came to the fields of Moab and they were there *settled for a short time.*

3. Elimelech, Naomi's husband, *who was weak of heart*, died.[8] She remained and her two sons. *Naomi remained strong of heart.*[9] *She raised her sons, but they, like their father, were weak of heart.*

    a. *Naomi said to Mahlon and Chilion, "Look, you two are like your father. You require each of you a helpmate, a woman who can attend to you. Now, see, I have gathered food from among the people of the plains of Moab and I have seen many young women, who are strong of heart like myself. There are nearby two young women, who are friends, from among the people of the land. Go now and find these women who are like me. And bring them to our home that they may attend you."*[10]

4. They lifted up for themselves Moabite wives, the name of one Orpah and the name of the second Ruth. *The women had strong hands and generous hearts, and they found favor in the eyes of their mother-in-law. They attended to the needs of their husbands.* They resided there about ten years. *But their husbands remained weak of heart, and they did not know them.*[11] *And their love was for their mother-in-law, and they were a comfort to one another.*[12]

5. The two of them, Mahlon and Chilion, also died. The woman remained without her sons and husband *and so, too, did her daughters-in-law. But while there was food in the plains of Moab they remained dwelling together, and they clung each to each other and they comforted one another during their time of mourning.*[13]

6. *And when their time of mourning was complete*, she got up and her daughters-in-law. She returned from the plains of Moab because she had heard the Eternal One paid attention to His [*sic*] people, giving them bread.

7. She went out from the place where she was and her two daughters-in-law with her. They walked in the road to return to the land of Judah.

8. Naomi said to her two daughters-in-law, "Go, return to the house of your mother. The Eternal One will do *hesed* with you as you did with the dead and with me. *Comforting me in my misery.*

9. May the Eternal One give to you [that you] find rest, [each] woman in the house of her husband." She kissed them and they lifted up their

voice and they cried *for they loved their mother-in-law and their desire was for her.*[14]

10. They said to her, "Certainly, we will return with you to your people."

11. Naomi said, "Return, my daughters. Why are you walking with me? Do I have more sons in my womb and they will become husbands for you?

12. Return there, my daughters, for I am too old to be with a man.[15] For if I said I have hope and also I was tonight with a man and also I gave birth to son,

13. Would you wait for them until they grew up? Would you shut yourself off from marriage in order not to be with a man? *For in a household of three women there is much comfort but no rest or security.*[16] No, my daughters, for I am more bitter than you because the hand of the Eternal One came out against me in *destroying my security.*"[17]

14. They lifted up their voices and they cried more. Orpah kissed her mother-in-law, but Ruth clung to her *as a man leaves his father and his mother and clings to his wife and they become as one flesh.*[18]

15. She said, "Here, be like your sister-in-law who has returned to her people and to her gods. Return after your sister-in-law *and find comfort with someone who is not me. For now I am too bitter to love you and seek your peace.*"[19]

16. Ruth said, "Do not entreat me to abandon you to return and be away from you, because wherever you go, I will go; and wherever you will rest overnight, I will rest overnight with you; your people, my people; and your God, my God.

17. Wherever you will die, I will die and there I will be buried. Thus the Eternal One will do to me and thus will add if anything but death will cause a separation between me and you."

18. She saw that she was determined to go with her. She refrained to speak with her, *though in her bitterness and distress she clung to Ruth.*[20]

19. The two of them[21] walked together *for seven days*[22] until they came to Bethlehem. When they came to Bethlehem, the whole city was in an uproar about them, *for Naomi had disguised herself as a man, the husband of Ruth, as they traveled from the plains of Moab to Bethlehem in order to protect them.*[23] *And travelers returning along the road said, "A Moabitess and her Ephramite husband travel towards Bethlehem." They did not know that Naomi was a woman. When Naomi and her daughter-in-law returned to Bethlehem*, they said, "Is this Naomi?" *for they saw what appeared to be a man, yet they believed to recognize their friend of long ago.*[24]

20. She said to them, "Don't call me Naomi. Call me 'Mara' ['bitter one'], because *the God who might have offered me a breast of comfort, but who destroys [Shaddai]*[25] provoked greatly against me *instead.*

21. I went full and the Eternal One has brought me back empty. *I went away a mother of two sons, and I return to you a husband to my daughter-in-law with no children.* Why do you call me Naomi? On the contrary the Eternal One answered me and *the God who might have offered me a breast of comfort but who destroys [Shaddai] instead* has dealt harshly with me."

22. Naomi returned and Ruth the Moabitess, her daughter-in-law, with her, returning from the plains of Moab.[26] And they, *Naomi like a husband and her daughter-in-law*,[27] came to Bethlehem at the beginning of the barley harvest.

Chapter 2

1. And to Naomi there was a relation of her husband's, a mighty man of valor, from the family of Elimelech, and his name was Boaz.

2. Ruth the Moabitess said to Naomi, "Please, may I go to the field and I will glean ears of grain? After that I will find favour in his eyes." She said to her, "Go, my daughter, *my bride.*[28] *Find favor in the eyes of another, for we cannot sustain ourselves on our own.*"[29]

3. She went; she came; she gleaned in the field behind the reapers. She chanced upon Boaz's portion of the field, he who was from the family of Elimelech.

4. Behold, Boaz came from Bethlehem. He said to the reapers, "The Eternal One is with you." They said to him, "The Eternal One bless you."

5. Boaz said to his young man, the head of the reapers, "*Just as you belong to me,*[30] to whom does this young woman belong?"

6. The young man, the head of the reapers *who belonged to Boaz*,[31] replied and he said, "The young woman is a Moabitess. She is the one who returned with Naomi from the plains of Moab.[32]

7. She said, 'Please may I reap and gather among the sheaves behind the reapers?' She came and she stood from the morning until now, resting in the house [but] a little."

8. Boaz said to Ruth, "Have you not heard, my daughter, do not go to glean in another field and also do not pass over from this and thus cling with my young girls.

9. [Keep] your eyes on the field which they are reaping. You will walk behind them. Have I not commanded the young men not to touch you? You will be thirsty and you will go to the vessels and you will drink from that which the young men have drawn."

10. She fell down on her face. She bowed to the ground. She said to him, "Why have I found favor in your eyes to pay attention to me and I am a foreigner?"

11. Boaz answered and he said to her, "It has surely been told to me every-
    thing that you did for your mother-in-law after the death of your hus-
    band. You left your father and your mother and the land of your birth
    and you clung to your mother-in-law.[33] You went to a people whom you
    did not know prior to three days ago.

12. The Eternal One will repay your work *and steadfast love.*[34] You will
    be completely recompensed by the Eternal One the God of Israel from
    whom you came to seek refuge under His [*sic*] wings."

13. She said, "I will find favor in your eyes, my lord, because you have
    comforted me and because you spoke from the heart to your maidser-
    vant and I am not even as one of your maidservants."

14. Boaz said to her at meal time, "Draw near hither. You will eat from the
    bread and you will dip your piece of bread in vinegar." She sat next to
    the reapers. He held out roasted grain to her. She ate and she was satis-
    fied and she had leftovers.

15. She arose to reap. Boaz commanded his young men saying, "Also
    between the sheaves she will reap and you will not abuse her.

16. And also you will draw out bundles of grain and you will leave them.
    She will reap and you will not rebuke her."

17. She reaped in the field until the evening. She beat out that which she
    reaped. It was about an ephah of barley.

18. She lifted it up and she came to the city. Her mother-in-law saw what
    she had reaped. She brought it out and she gave her *that in addition to*[35]
    that which she had left over from her being sated.

19. Her mother-in-law said to her, "Where did you reap today? And where
    did you work? Let the one be blessed who recognized you." She told
    her mother-in-law with whom she had worked. She said, "The name of
    the man with whom I worked today is Boaz."

20. Naomi said to her daughter-in-law, "Blessed be the Eternal One *and
    blessed be Boaz,*[36] who did not forsake his *hesed* to the living and to
    the dead." Naomi said to her, "The man is close to us; he is one of our
    redeemers."

21. Ruth the Moabitess also said, "For he said to me, 'Cling to the young
    men who are mine until they have finished all of my harvest.'"

22. Naomi said to Ruth, her daughter-in-law, "It is good, my daughter,
    because you will go out with his young women and they will not be
    hostile with you in another field."

23. She clung to Boaz's young women to glean until finishing the
    barley harvest and harvesting the wheat. She remained with her
    mother-in-law.

Chapter 3

1. Naomi, her mother-in-law, said to her, "My daughter, *have you not been better to me than sons, but we are two widows alone.*[37] *Therefore should I not protect us*[38] *and* shall I not seek for you rest that will be good for you and for me as well?

2. And now, is not Boaz one who is known to us, *in whose eyes you have found favor and* you were with his young women. Behold, he is winnowing barley on the threshing floor tonight.

3. Wash, anoint, and put on your dress. You will go down[39] to the threshing room floor *and I will be with you in your heart.*[40] Don't make yourself known to the man until he has finished to eat and drink.

4. And it will be in his lying down; you will know the place where he will lie there. You will come. You will uncover at the place of his feet and you will lie down[41] *and I will be with you in your heart*[42] and he will tell you what to do."

5. She said to her, "Everything you will say to me, I will do, *that we may be secure with the man.*"[43]

6. She went down to the threshing floor. She did according to everything her mother-in-law commanded her.

7. Boaz ate. He drank. His heart was happy. He went to lie down at the edge of the heap of grain. She came secretly. She uncovered at the place of his feet. She lay down.

8. It came to pass at midnight, the man was *trembling* {and his flesh became soft like a [boiled] turnip}.[44] He was grasped and behold a woman was lying at the place of his feet.

9. He said, "Who are you?" She said, "I am Ruth, your maidservant. You will spread out your wing over your maidservant {by taking me to wife}[45] *along with my mother-in-law, who counseled me this night and who sought my rest and to whom I am sworn,* because you are *our*[46] redeemer."

10. He said, "Blessed are you to the Eternal One, my daughter. You have acted benevolently; the last of your *hesed* is greater than the first in not going after young men whether poor or rich.

11. And now, my daughter, do not fear, all that you will say I will do for you because all [who sit at] the gate of my people know you are a woman of valor *and so, too, your mother-in-law.*

12. And now, because truly I am a redeemer but there is also another redeemer closer than me.

13. Stay overnight tonight. It will be in the morning, if he will redeem you good, he will redeem. And if he will not desire to redeem you, I, I will redeem you, as the Eternal One lives. Lie down until morning."

14. She lay down at the place of his feet until the morning. She got up before a man will recognize his friend. He said, "Do not make it known that the woman came to the threshing floor."

15. He said, "Bring the cloak that is on you and grasp it." She grasped it. He measured six barleys. He put it on *her saying, "Do not go empty-handed to your mother-in-law for she too has found favour in my eyes."*[47] He went to the city.

16. She went to her mother-in-law. She said, "Who are you, my daughter? *Do you still belong to me or to the man?"*[48] *Ruth replied, "I belong to you and to him. I have sworn that nothing shall part us and so it shall be."*[49] And she told her everything the man had done for her.

17. She said, "These six barleys he gave me for he said, 'Do not go empty to your mother-in-law *for she, too, has found favor in my eyes for her good counsel of you.'"*[50]

18. She said, "Sit with me, my daughter, until you will know how the matter will fall because the man will not be still until the matter is finished today."

Chapter 4

1. And Boaz went up to the gate. He sat there and, behold, the redeemer, whom Boaz spoke of, passed by. He said, "Turn aside and sit here, Ploni Almoni." He turned aside. He sat.

2. He took ten men from the elders of the city. He said, "Sit here." They sat.

3. *Now Boaz had spoken with Naomi about a field, which belonged to Elimelech.* He said to the redeemer, "A portion of the field, which belongs to our brother, Elimelech, Naomi is selling it, having now returned from the plains of Moab.

4. And I, I said, I will let you know,[51] saying, 'Purchase,' in the presence of the ones sitting and in the presence of the elders of my people. If you will redeem, redeem; and if he[52] will not redeem, tell me and I will know. For if there's no one to redeem, then I am after you." He said, "I will redeem."

5. Boaz said, "On the day of your purchase of the field from the hand of Naomi and from Ruth, the Moabitess, the wife of the deceased, you have acquired her to cause to raise up the name of the deceased on his inheritance *and her mother-in-law, too.*"[53]

6. The redeemer said, "I am not able to redeem for myself lest I destroy my own inheritance, you redeem for yourself my redemption for I am not able to redeem."

7. And this was what was done previously in Israel about redemption and recompense to establish every matter: a man pulled off his sandal and gave it to his friend and this was the method of attestation in Israel.

8. The redeemer said to Boaz, "Purchase for yourself." And he pulled off his sandal.

9. Boaz said to the elders and all the people, "You are witnesses today for I have purchased everything that was Elimelech's and everything that was Chilion's and Mahlon's from Naomi, *including her for a wife, though she has no more sons in her, in order that she may find rest.*[54]

10. And also Ruth the Moabitess, the wife of Mahlon, I have purchased for myself for a wife to establish the name of the dead upon his inheritance, and the name of the dead will not be cut off from among his brothers or his estate.[55] You are witnesses today."

11. All the people who were in the gate and the elders said, "We are witnesses. Let the Eternal One make the woman, *Ruth*,[56] who comes to your house be like Rachel and like Leah, the two of whom built up the house of Israel, and make valor in Ephrathah and make for yourself a name in Bethlehem.

12. Let your house be like the house of Perez, whom Tamar bore to Judah, from the seed that the Eternal One will give to you from this young woman."

13. Boaz took Ruth. She was a wife to him. He came to her. The Eternal One gave to her pregnancy. She gave birth to a son. *Boaz took Naomi. She was a wife to him, though she had no more sons in her womb.*[57]

14. The women said to Naomi, "Blessed be the Eternal One who did not withhold from you a redeemer today. His name will be exclaimed in Israel.

15. He will be to you a reviving soul and sustain your old age because your daughter-in-law, who loves you, bore him, she who is better to you than seven sons. *And your husband, Boaz, who loves you, fathered him, he who cares for you in your old age.*"[58]

   a. *Ruth said, "Take this boy that we may raise him together." Boaz said, "Take this boy, for he is the son of our family."*[59]

16. Naomi took the boy. She laid him on her chest. She was to him a foster parent/wet nurse.

17. The women neighbors called him a name saying, "A son is born to Naomi *and Ruth and Boaz.*"[60] They called his name Obed, he was the father of Jesse, the father of David.

18. These are the generations of Perez. Perez begat Hezron.

19. And Hezron begat Ram and Ram begat Aminadab.

20. And Aminadab begat Nahshon and Nahshon begat Salmon.
21. And Salmon begat Boaz and Boaz begat Obed.
22. And Obed begat Jesse and Jesse begat David, *who knew the love of men and women alike.*[61]

NOTES

1. Simon G. D. A. Lasair, "Targum and Translation: A New Approach to a Classic Problem," *AJS Review* 34, no. 2 (2010): 275. Italics original.

2. Translation from https://www.sefaria.org/Aramaic_Targum_to_Ruth.1.1 ?lang=bi.

3. For more on the text of the Targum to Ruth, see D. R. G. Beattie, "The Textual Tradition of Targum Ruth," in *The Aramaic Bible: Targums in the Historical Context*, edited by D. R. G. Beattie and M. J. McNamara (Sheffield: Sheffield Academic Press, 1994).

4. The translation is my own. It is deliberately fairly literal, which may make it feel somewhat labored (though I hope not distractingly so) and which is similar to many Targum translations in English.

5. Some of the Targumim are named after the author (or mistakenly identified author) of the translation (e.g., Onkelos, Jonathan, and Pseudo-Jonathan). For lack of a better idea, I have, therefore, decided to name this Targum after myself.

6. Cf. Judg. 21:25. I wanted to reinforce this idea from the end of the Book of Judges that the Book of Ruth is set during a time without consistent leadership, when individuals needed to make the best choices for themselves, which would not be in accordance with what we might perceive of as biblical norms.

7. As distinct from the commentary at the end of Ruth Rabbah 1:4, which seeks to place blame on Elimelech himself as a means of explaining his subsequent death:

Why was Elimelech punished? Because he struck [despair] into the hearts of Israel, for nothing did he rule the country, and the countrymen were sure that when the years of plague/famine would come, he would be able to sustain the country for 10 years with food! When the year of famine came to the land, his maid went to the market stalls and her basket was in her hand, and the people of the district said: "Is this the one whom we trusted in that when the famine came he would be able to provide for us for ten years? And see! His maid is standing in the market and her basket is in her hand!" Elimelech was one the great leaders of his district and one of the financial supporters of his generation. But when the years of famine came, he said, "Now all Israel will come knocking at my door, each one with his basket." He got up and fled from them. This is the meaning of the verse, "and a man went [out] from Bethlehem in Judah." (https://www.sefaria.org /Ruth_Rabbah.1?ven=Sefaria_Community_Translation&vhe=Midrash_Rabbah_--_TE &lang=bi)

I have included this insertion in order to remove any blame from any of the members of the family for the tragedies that befall them.

8. I have used the term "weak of heart" here to encompass both physical and mental well-being.

9. As discussed previously, I have used the term "strong of heart" to encompass both physical and mental well-being. I wanted to make more explicit what is already implicit in the biblical text. Whereas the rest of the family cannot survive the harsh conditions of famine and displacement, Naomi is clearly better able to withstand the adversities she is forced to endure. She survives the famine in Bethlehem, the long journey through harsh country from Bethlehem to Moab, and whatever privations the family may have faced as migrants in Moab. Such a woman, who is both physically and mentally robust, may suggest characteristics more commonly associated with masculinity—physical strength and endurance, resilience, determination, and grit, for example. See chapter 4 in this book, "Who Is Naomi?"

10. This insertion, which is substantive and could be understood as an additional verse, makes explicit a reason why Mahlon and Chilion required wives. Rather than the more typical biblical, heteropatriarchal marriage for the purpose of procreation and continuation of the family line, Mahlon and Chilion, whose very names signpost their poor health, require wives who will be caretakers for them. These wives will, therefore, require the same physical robustness and mental fortitude that Naomi displays.

11. Assuming Mahlon and Chilion are generally in poor health, we should not be surprised that they are unable to impregnate their wives. But in comparison to Ruth 4:13, where the text makes explicit not only that Boaz marries Ruth but also that he has sexual intercourse with her, the Masoretic text of Ruth 1:4:4 never states anything more than that Mahlon and Chilion "lifted up" Ruth and Orpah. Based on this intertextual comparison, I am extrapolating further that sexual intercourse never occurs between Mahlon-Ruth and Chilion-Orpah.

12. As women working together in a household where the men are weak, ill, or (in the case of Elimelech) dead, Naomi, Ruth, and Orpah would naturally have had to become reliant on each other. I am explicitly stating, however, that more than simply reliance, they develop a relationship of mutual affection, love, and concern for each other. I have deliberately used the word "love" in this insertion to reflect Ruth 4:15. Whether the relationship between the three women as described in this insertion might also have a sexual dimension is not explicitly stated here but could easily be understood to be implied.

13. The Masoretic text is unclear on how long the women remained in Moab following the deaths of Mahlon and Chilion. I wanted to open the possibility that Naomi, Ruth, and Orpah may have had time to develop their relationship without the presence of men. Because the Hebrew Bible is less specific about the length of mourning periods than later halachic developments, I have left the specific length of the period ambiguous so as not to appear anachronistic. Nevertheless, a mourning period of whatever length would have been normal and would have afforded the women some time together on their own to continue to develop the bonds between them.

Additionally, I have used the word "clung" as an intertextual allusion to Ruth 1:14. See notes 21–22 in chapter 2, "Ruth 1: The Arrangement and Rearrangement of Families," for more on the use of the root ד.ב.ק.

14. Here I have further developed what is more obliquely referred to in verse 4. Not only do Ruth and Orpah love Naomi, but they also desire her, suggesting explicitly both a physical and an emotional relationship. Although kissing in the Hebrew Bible has a range of implications, not all of which are sexual in nature, I felt that adding Ruth and Orpah's desire for Naomi here, after the Masoretic text describes them kissing, flowed better and suggested that their relationship had developed over time.

15. Cf. Doniger, *The Bedtrick*, 261: "But Naomi is too old, as the Hebrew literally puts it, to 'be with a man' or 'for or of a man'—that is, to attract a husband."

16. Naomi is making a statement of fact in the heteropatriarchal society of the Hebrew Bible rather than making a judgment about her relationship with Ruth and Orpah. But I have also purposely clarified that the relationship is between the three of them, not two separate dyadic relationships existing within their single household.

17. Naomi is clarifying that her bitterness is not because of Ruth and Orpah and their relationship, but rather that within heteropatriarchal biblical society, security must be obtained through a male relative.

18. Cf. Gen. 2:24: עַל־כֵּן יַעֲזָב־אִישׁ אֶת־אָבִיו וְאֶת־אִמּוֹ וְדָבַק בְּאִשְׁתּוֹ וְהָיוּ לְבָשָׂר אֶחָד׃

Therefore a man leaves his father and his mother and clings to his wife and they become as one flesh.

Although the root דבק does not always connate sexual desire/union, the allusion to Gen. 2:24 is very strong. Adding in the insertion reinforces the intertextual reference, making a strong case for a sexual relationship as well as emotional relationship between Ruth and Naomi. See "From Triads to Dyads (Ruth 1:14–22)" in chapter 2 for a more complete analysis of this term.

19. With this insertion, I have tried to shed some light on Naomi's emotional state, which would help to elucidate why in verse 18 she does not overtly reply to Ruth's declaration in verses 15–16.

20. This insertion imagines what Naomi might have done, rather than what she did not say, in response to Ruth.

21. Note that the Hebrew pronoun here is שְׁתֵּיהֶם (*Sǝtêhem*), "two of them," which is grammatically masculine. More normally in Biblical Hebrew, we would expect to find the masculine plural employed only when women appear in a group that also contains men. I am using this "misgendering" of the two women as a hint to my insertion in this verse (i.e., the notion that Naomi could have disguised herself as a man for the journey).

Also see Stephanie Day Powell, *Narrative Desire and the Book of Ruth* (London: T&T Clark, 2018), 50:

Additionally, seven times (1:7 twice, 1:9, 1:11, 1:13, 1:19b and 4:11) there is a curious subject-verb anomaly in the Hebrew in which the masculine verb ending appears where the referent is two females. . . . At the very least, these incongruities suggest awareness, barely supressed below the narrative's surface, of the constructed and mutable nature of gender and gender roles.

22. Seven days is a reasonable estimate of the time required to walk from Moab to Bethlehem. Though the actual distance is not extensive (approximately thirty miles), according to Koosed, "The Dead Sea lies between the two lands [Moab and

Bethlehem] at 1,329 feet below sea level, the lowest point on earth. Ruth and Naomi had to descend 4,329 feet to cross the Dead Sea and then ascent 3,679 feet into the Judean hill country" (Koosed, *Gleaning Ruth*, 22). But seven days is also a highly symbolic number biblically, signifying a period of completion or a full cycle. Taken in conjunction with the possibility of Naomi and Ruth posing as a married couple, with Naomi dressing as a man during their journey, it suggests a significant period of time in which Naomi and Ruth could behave both privately and publicly as though they were in a relationship with each other.

23. In Gen. 20 and 26, Sarah and Rebekah, respectively, disguise themselves as the sisters of their husbands rather than wives in order to protect them from danger in foreign lands. Although we have no examples of women dressing as men in order to protect themselves, given the dangers to women traveling without male company, it does not seem far-fetched to suggest that dressing as a man might be an effective strategy for Naomi to protect both herself and Ruth. Additionally, dressing and acting as a man with a wife would have allowed Naomi an opportunity to publicly express masculine behaviors. Finally, although Deut. 22:5 does expressly outlaw the practice of cross-dressing for both men and women, Deut. 23:4 also expressly forbids marriage to a Moabite. If the Book of Ruth can transgress one of these laws, then it does not seem unreasonable that it might break others. Cf. Guest, "Troubling the Waters," 47 note 4.

24. The possibility of Naomi dressing as a man makes for a different reading of the reaction of the women of Bethlehem to Naomi. They literally would not have been able to reconcile the figure they saw before them, who dresses and behaves as a man, with the woman who left Bethlehem more than ten years prior. The insertions in this verse allow for a reading of a genderfluid or transgender Naomi, who goes away as a married woman with children and returns as a man with a wife.

25. This insertion plays with the possible meanings of שַׁדַּי (*Shaddai*), the etymology of which is contested. Two of the possible roots are שׁ.ד.ד. (*Šdd*; destroy) and שַׁד (*Šad*; breast). Knauf suggests that "Shadday is re-etymologized by the root SDD. This understanding of the name may also have influenced the use of Shadday (as the 'violent/powerful' god) in Ruth 1:20–21" (Knauf, "Shadday," 1419). For a comprehensive discussion of the etymology term שׁדי, see Steins, "שׁדי/*sadday*," 420–24. See also Queen-Sutherland, *Ruth and Esther*, 64.

26. I have translated עמה simply as "with her." Schipper translates it both here and in verse 7 as "under her authority" (Schipper, *The Anchor Yale Bible: Ruth*, 79, 85–86, 106, and 110). If Schipper is correct, the use of עמה signifies a power imbalance between Naomi and Ruth, with Naomi having power over Ruth just as a husband would have power/authority over the members of his household, particularly his wife/wives and daughter/s. Schipper's translation could give greater weight to the idea of Naomi fulfilling the role of husband.

27. The pronoun הֵמָּה (*hēmmāh*) is masculine, despite the antecedents both being female, Naomi and Ruth. Schipper cites this usage as "an example of a gender-neutralized pronoun" (Schipper, *The Anchor Yale Bible: Ruth*, 111). This insertion, however, employing the previous idea of Naomi dressing as a man, suggests that the reason for the use of the male pronoun is that Naomi is presenting as male at this point in the story. Where a man is part of any group, even were the group predominantly made up of women, Biblical Hebrew genders the entire group as male grammatically.

28. Cf. Cant. 4:9, 10, 12; 5:1, which uses the phrase "my sister, my bride" in reference to the female lover.

29. Ruth is asking Naomi's permission to go reaping, presumably because they are in need of substance, though at no point does the text state overtly that they are going hungry in Bethlehem, and in Chapter 4, we discover that Naomi owns a field of her own from the estate of Elimelech. But Ruth is also asking whether she may go to find favor in "his" eyes, though she does not state whose eyes.

This insertion allows Naomi to acknowledge her affection/love for Ruth in addition to giving her explicit permission to find favor in the eyes of another, particularly a male other, which in the heteropatriarchal world of the Bible was necessary for the women's long-term survival.

30. This insertion is based on Pyper's speculation on the relationship of Boaz to the young men who work in his fields (Pyper, "Boaz Reawakened," 452–53). Pyper suggests that Boaz may have homosexual relationships with the young men working in his field, perhaps especially the head of the reapers.

31. See prior note. The repetition of this insertion reinforces the nature of the relationship.

32. Cf. West, "Ruth," who translates the reply of the head of the reapers as "She belongs to Naomi" (192).

33. Perhaps Boaz recognizes a kindred spirit (i.e., someone who is capable of clinging to a member of the same sex). If, as Pyper speculates, Boaz is involved in a same-sex relationship with one or more of the young men who work in his field, then he may feel more positively and protectively toward a woman in a similar position.

34. Without the insertion, this verse could feel economically transactional, rather than emotionally connected. The insertion is designed to counteract that effect as well as to reinforce Ruth's emotional connection to Naomi.

35. Without the insertion, this verse could read as though Ruth were *only* giving Naomi leftovers and that Ruth cared more for her own full belly than for Naomi's. This insertion suggests instead that Ruth gave Naomi what she had reaped as well as her own leftovers, making Ruth appear more generous and concerned for Naomi's well-being.

36. The antecedent of the personal pronominal suffix is variously understood to be a reference to either God or Boaz. This insertion helps clarify that Boaz is the clear antecedent. For more on this debate, see "Ruth 2:20" in chapter 6 of this book.

37. The language of "better than sons" is an echo of Ruth 4:15, but it also reinforces the vulnerability of the two widowed women living alone together and the inherent instability of their relationship, particularly in the heteropatriarchal biblical world.

38. Without the insertions, Naomi's speech in this verse refers only to Ruth. This insertion and the one at the end of the verse clarify Naomi's intentions—that she is seeking a situation that will suit both of their needs and make both of them more secure. Whether that sentiment is implicit in the text and whether Ruth understands that point is a subject of debate, particularly regarding how manipulative Naomi is in this verse. By making her intentions more overt, these insertions suggest a more open and honest relationship between Naomi and Ruth.

39. *Ketiv*: *I will go down.*

40. This insertion plays on the *qere ketiv* and suggests that Naomi understands the risks she is asking Ruth to take and is offering support as well as instructions.

41. *Ketiv*: *I will lie down.*

42. See note 40.

43. This insertion clarifies that Ruth understands fully and properly the constraints of the heteropatriarchy in which she and Naomi must function.

44. In part, I have retained this targumic insertion because of its humor. It simply lightens the mood. It also signifies that Boaz was not automatically turned on by Ruth's (or, indeed, any stranger's) presence in the middle of the night. Alongside the fear of the Masoretic text, it suggests that there is something awkward, even perhaps misplaced, about Ruth's approach to Boaz in this fashion. He is not so randy that anyone turning up in the middle of the night next to him is assumed to be a sexual partner. Boaz's fear and physical response of limpness hint rather at some prior negative experience. (Targum translation from https://www.sefaria.org/Aramaic_Targum_to_Ruth.3.8?lang=bi.)

45. The targumic insertion makes Ruth's intentions clear—namely, that she is not seeking sexual relations but marriage, which was not at all clear from the manner of her approach to Boaz. My additional insertion, alongside the targumic one, is the most direct reference to the possibility of a polyamorous family (though the reading does not demand it; it could simply be understood as creating a polygamous family, which in this case would have been entirely legal within the biblical framework). Ruth not only suggests overtly that Boaz take both herself and Naomi in marriage but also attempts to make a good account of Naomi. Ruth does so by explaining that Naomi has engineered the event and has done so with caring intentions (quoting from 3:1), thereby trying to persuade Boaz of Naomi's worthiness. Ruth also makes clear that she has an obligation to Naomi (stemming from 1:15–16), which requires her to remain with Naomi. (Targum translation from https://www.sefaria.org/Aramaic_Targum_to_Ruth.3.9?lang=bi&with=all&lang2=en.)

46. Cf. Ruth 2:20, in which Naomi refers to Boaz as *our* redeemer.

47. In this insertion, Boaz accepts Naomi's good intentions in sending Ruth to him on the threshing room floor and suggests that he will be willing to protect Naomi as well, through marriage.

48. Naomi's question in this insertion suggests that she believes at this stage that Ruth will have to choose between herself and Boaz. Ruth may be able to think beyond dyads, but Naomi has not yet caught up.

49. Ruth corrects Naomi's dyadic assumption in this insertion, making it plain that she can be in a relationship with both of them and committed to two people simultaneously.

50. Only at the point at which Ruth gives Naomi Boaz's gift does she reveal in this insertion that Naomi, too, has found favor with Boaz and the reason why. Although she does not state overtly that Boaz intends to marry them both, the implication is there.

51. Literally, "reveal to your ear."

52. Most Hebrew manuscripts alongside Septuagint and Targum read "he" here (NJPS, 1747 note a). However, many English translations, including NJPS, render "you."

53. This insertion simply clarifies whom Boaz intends to marry. Although marrying both women certainly does not conform to the rules of levirate marriage, neither, strictly speaking, does the Masoretic version of Ruth (without this insertion). Suggesting that Boaz includes a proposal to marry Naomi as well in his discussions with *Peloni Almoni* does further complicate an already complicated matter, but I see no reason why that should be an obstacle to the possibility.

54. This insertion explains Boaz's rationale for also taking Naomi for a wife.

55. Literally, "the gate of his place."

56. Simply added for clarity in light of the insertions suggesting that Boaz took Naomi, too, in marriage.

57. Echoing the language as used about Boaz's marriage to Ruth, this insertion makes overt that Boaz married Naomi and explains why they had no children, referring back to Naomi's own statement on the subject in Ruth 1:11.

58. Again, the language of this insertion deliberately echoes what the women say about Ruth's relationship to Naomi, creating a parallelism between the Hebrew original and the English insertion.

59. In the Masoretic text, no reason is given for why Naomi is handed the baby. Although the women understand that Ruth has actually borne the infant, Naomi appears to simply take the baby away and place him at her breast. This insertion gives voice to both Ruth and Boaz, who in the Masoretic text no longer have any voice (Ruth disappears altogether, and Boaz is only mentioned as part of the genealogy at the end of the story). Instead, this insertion not only explains why Naomi took the baby but also makes the will of both Ruth and Boaz clear. Furthermore, this insertion exemplifies how the three of them together might be seen to form a family.

60. Following from the previous insertion, adding both Ruth and Boaz here clarifies that they are all jointly the parents of Obed, a radical departure from the Masoretic text and the most overt reference to the polyamorous family in this "Targum."

61. The reference here is to David's relationship with his numerous wives as well as Jonathan, suggesting that being the descendant of a polyamorous family may have enabled him to view more expansively the possibilities for whom and how he could love.

Conclusion

I began this study with the suggestion that this book would be another spark off the hammer that shatters the rock of the text, revealing something as of yet unexpressed in the interpretative pantheon. I believe that by beginning with reading Ruth for relationships, just not necessarily dyadic ones, I have established a number of previously unexplored possibilities within the Book of Ruth. In reading not only as a trained Bible scholar but also as a rabbi, I have listened to the potent lacunae in the text, focusing on what is *not* said as much as on what *is* said. Finally, I have created a fully expressed *davar acher* in the contemporary Targum that concludes this book, imaginatively engaging through a detailed reading deeply rooted in the biblical text to reveal what might be lurking beneath the surface if only we attune our ears differently.

The Book of Ruth has long been seen as a sort of romantic idyll, whether by readers invested in a hetero- or homonormative reading of the text. Ruth is either about the Ruth–Boaz relationship or the Ruth-Naomi one—ultimately, I argue, pulling the story apart in unsatisfactory ways. But in reading for a triadic resolution to the story, these apparently conflicting tensions can be resolved in a more holistic fashion that is also textually supported. As I have explored, acts of *hesed* stand together with the narrative of marriage and redemption to offer a substantive clue that Naomi, Ruth, and Boaz are inseparable from one another.

The three of them could have simply settled for a biblically normative patriarchal polygamous relationship. There is nothing radical in suggesting such a resolution, and biblical law would not prevent such a union (i.e., Boaz marrying both Ruth and Naomi).[1] But the text does not tell us that this is what happened, where it so easily might have. No biblical laws prevent a mother-in-law and daughter-in-law, both widowed, from marrying again or marrying the same man. Yet this ending is *not* the one that the biblical text overtly expresses.

In asking the implied question, "Why not?" I have tried to open up the space for exploring what might be hidden beneath the surface of the text. Ruth plainly commits herself to Naomi in perpetuity (Ruth 1:16–17). Ruth also marries Boaz (Ruth 4:13), an outcome not merely approved of but actively engineered *by Naomi* (Ruth 3:1–4) for the women's mutual benefit. Ruth clearly bears a male child to Boaz, and yet the women of Bethlehem proclaim this child to be the son of Naomi (Ruth 4:17). These hints, alongside the many other clues littered throughout the text, suggest strongly that trying to divide the story into a series of dyadic relationships does not satisfactorily explain what is happening here.

In my interpretation of Ruth 1, I expound that already in the Ruth–Orpah–Naomi dynamic, we find an early indication of the importance of triadic relationships in this story. In table 6.1, I lay out the ways in which *hesed* intertwines Ruth, Naomi, and Boaz. Probing why *both* levirate marriage *and* redemption are prominently included in Ruth 4, I demonstrate how both are important for creating relationships between Boaz, Naomi, and Ruth. All of these clues, alongside other hints about gender identity and sexual orientation, lead me toward a triadic resolution to the narrative.

So why is the articulation of such a resolution so rare and hidden? Yes, clues in the text suggest a polyamorous polygamous relationship in which Boaz, Naomi, and Ruth commit to a union of polyfidelity within a space of mutual respect and support for one another. And yet, within the dominant heteropatriarchal world of the Hebrew Bible, although such a relationship was possible, it was still too subversive to name it overtly.

Each of the main figures—Naomi, Ruth, and Boaz—offers clues to an identity encoded within the text that may have been considered unconventional and problematic in mainstream society. Ruth, perhaps, is the most obvious as a proscribed Moabitess, but more obliquely, her sexual orientation appears to align most closely with what we today might term bisexuality or, alternatively, pansexuality.[2] Boaz, as Pyper so expertly uncovers, may be most comfortable in homonormative spaces, but he must also exist within a wider community that expects him to perform as a heteropatriarchal man, married to a woman (or women) and produce a male heir. Naomi is, in many respects, the most ambiguous figure of the three, shifting her gender presentation throughout the narrative and thus signifying a gender nonconforming person.

In a polyamorous polygamous resolution to the story, each of these characters has the space to be themselves safely within a supportive relationship and wider environment. They can live out a life of *hesed* and blessing together. Together they can raise the product of this "work," their son Obed. The text provides a model and a proof text for a polyamorous relationship of comper-sion: moreover, a relationship depicted as approved of—even celebrated and blessed by—the wider community, as stated by both the male elders at the gate and the women of Bethlehem. As such, the story also opens up possibili-ties of legitimation, happiness, and acceptance for polyamorous relationships in the present, particularly for people whose religious practice centers on the Hebrew Bible as a sacred text.

Of course, the designation of polyamory can only be anachronistic in this context, but that does not preclude it from being an accurate description of the Naomi-Boaz-Ruth relationship. Because a term was not coined in the biblical period does not mean that the meaning it encapsulates did not exist in previous times. Moreover, the use of this term is important because, as a practicing rabbi, I am acutely aware that language matters to the lives of real people. Although this short monograph may have limited a readership within academic biblical studies circles, my hope is that the ideas contained within it permeate beyond the rarefied realms of the academy.

As Carleen Mandolfo has written so eloquently and importantly,

> The current social wars raging over biblical interpretations should make it clear that the choices we make about reading have political consequences as significant as those we make in the voting booth or with our checkbook. Our reading practices, in part, construct the symbolic world we inhabit and serve to motivate and justify our actions. Because words, particularly biblical words, possess the power to muster armies, we must approach the text with a certain ethical consciousness.[3]

To conceive of a biblical text that might present a polyamorous polygamous family in which each of the members of the union can safely express their sexual orientation and gender presentation and in which a child can be raised with legitimacy, so much so that he can be the ancestor of a king, is to cre-ate a world today in which polyamorous families and their progeny can be accepted without question into our own contemporary communities. Much as with the pioneering work of scholars and theologians who have shaped the space for feminist and queer people in biblical studies, to whom I owe an immeasurable debt of gratitude because without their work this study would not and could not exist, my sincerest hope is that this contribution will open up space for polyamorous families within my own tradition and potentially for others for whom the biblical text is sacred.

The way we tell and interpret stories matters, because stories shape the way we live in the world. Biblical stories, as the rabbis of the Talmud would say, על אחת כמה וכמה, "how much the more so." My Targum is, therefore, for me, the pinnacle of this volume, as it is my way of telling the story as a story, not "merely" offering an interpretation. Perhaps some synagogue, maybe even one of the ones at which I currently pray, will be able to read my Targum as the "translation" during the festival of Shavuot, when the Book of Ruth is read aloud in Jewish communities.

NOTES

1. Although biblical law does forbid marrying two sisters (Lev. 18:18) or a mother and daughter (Lev. 18:17), no such prohibition exists in regard to a mother-in-law and daughter-in-law.

2. Pansexuality means being sexually or romantically attracted to a person regardless of their gender identity or biological sex.

3. Mandolfo, *Daughter Zion Talks Back to the Prophets*, 27.

Bibliography

Adelman, Rachel E. *The Female Ruse: Women's Deception & Divine Sanction in the Hebrew Bible*. Sheffield: Sheffield Phoenix Press, 2017.

Adler, Rachel. *Engendering Judaism: An Inclusive Theology and Ethics*. Philadelphia: Jewish Publication Society, 1998.

Allarakha, Shaziya. "What Are the 72 Other Genders?" Accessed February 2, 2022. https://www.medicinenet.com/what_are_the_72_other_genders/article.htm

Alpert, Rebekah. "Finding Our Past: A Lesbian Interpretation of the Book of Ruth." In *Reading Ruth: Contemporary Women Reclaim a Sacred Story*, edited by Judith A. Kates and Gail Twersky Reimer, 91–96. New York: Ballantine Books, 1996.

Apostolacus, Katherine. "The Bible and The Transgender Christian: Mapping Transgender Hermeneutics in the 21st Century." *Journal of the Bible and its Reception* 5, no. 1 (2018): 1–29.

Bal, Mieke. *Lethal Love: Feminist Literary Readings of Biblical Love Stories*. Bloomington: Indiana University Press, 1987.

———. "The Rape of Narrative and Narrative of Rape." In *Literature and the Body: Essays on Populations and Persons*, edited by Elaine Scarry. Baltimore, MD: Johns Hopkins University Press, 1988.

Barker, Meg-John. "57 Genders (and None for Me?)—Part Two." Last updated March 11, 2020. https://www.open.edu/openlearn/society/politics-policy-people/society-matters/57-genders-and-none-me-part-two

Beattie, D. R. G. "The Textual Tradition of Targum Ruth." In *The Aramaic Bible: Targums in the Historical Context*, edited by D. R. G. Beattie and M. J. McNamara. Sheffield: Sheffield Academic Press, 1994.

Ben Ze'ev, Aaron. "'I Am Glad That My Partner Is Happy with Her Lover': On Jealousy and Compersion." In *The Moral Psychology of Love*, edited by Arina Pismenny and Berit Bogaard, 127–50. Lanham, MD: Rowman & Littlefield, 2022.

Berquist, Jon L. "Role Differentiation in the Book of Ruth." *Journal for the Study of the Old Testament* 57 (1993): 23–37.

Biala, Tamar, ed. *Dirshuni: Contemporary Women's Midrash*. Waltham, MA: Brandeis University Press, 2022.

Blyth, Caroline. *The Narrative of Rape in Genesis 34: Interpreting Dinah's Silence*. Oxford: Oxford University Press, 2010.

Botterwick, G. Johannes. "עָדָי." In *The Theological Dictionary of the Old Testament Vol V חמר-יהוה (hmr-YHWH)*, edited by G. Johannes Botterwick and Helmer Ringgen, 448–81. Grand Rapids, MI: William B. Eerdmans, 1986.

Brenner, Athalya. *I Am . . . Biblical Women Tell Their Own Stories*. Minneapolis, MN: Fortress Press, 1985.

Chu, Julie Li-Chuan. "Returning Home: The Inspiration of the Role Differentiation in the Book of Ruth for Taiwanese Women." In *Reading the Bible as Women: Perspectives from Africa, Asia, and Latin America* (Semeia 78), edited by Katherine Doob Sakenfeld and Sharon H. Ringe, 47–53. Atlanta: SBL, 1997.

Clark, Gordon R. *The Word Hesed in the Hebrew Bible*. Sheffield: Sheffield Academic Press, 1993.

Clines, David J. A., ed. *The Dictionary of Classical Hebrew Vol VI ס – פ*. Sheffield: Sheffield Phoenix Press, 2007.

Clines, David. "Why Is There a Song of Songs and What Does It Do to You If You Read It?" In *Interested Parties: The Ideology of Writers and Readers of the Hebrew Bible*, 94–121. Sheffield: Sheffield Academic Press, 1995.

Cornwall, Susannah, ed. *Intersex, Theology, and the Bible: Troubling Bodies in Church, Text, and Society*. Palgrave Macmillan, 2016.

Cowley, Arthur Ernest, and Emil Kautzsch. *Gesenius' Hebrew Grammar*. Oxford: Clarendon Press, 1910.

DeBlosi, Rabbi Nikki. "Toward a New Framework for Reform Jewish Views on Polyamory." *Reform Jewish Quarterly* (Fall 2022): 76–92.

Donaldson, Laura E. "The Sign of Orpah: Reading Ruth Through Native Eyes." In *A Feminist Companion to the Bible: Ruth and Esther (Second Series)*, edited by Athayla Brenner, 130–44. Sheffield: Sheffield Academic Press, 1999.

Doniger, Wendy. *The Bedtrick: Tales of Sex and Masquerade*. Chicago: University of Chicago Press, 2000.

Duncan, Celena M. "The Book of Ruth: On Boundaries, Love, and Truth." In *Take Back the Word: A Queer Reading of the Bible*, edited by Robert E. Goss and Mona West, 92–102. Cleveland, OH: Pilgrim Press, 2000.

Ebeling, Jennie R. *Women's Lives in Biblical Times*. London: T & T Clark, 2010.

Eskenazi, Tamara Cohn, and Tikva Frymer-Kensky. *The JPS Bible Commentary: Ruth*. Philadelphia: JPS, 2011.

Exum, J. Cheryl. *Art as Biblical Commentary: Visual Criticism from Hagar the Wife of Abraham to Mary the Mother of Jesus*. London: T&T Clark, 2019.

———. *Fragmented Women: Feminist (Sub)versions of Biblical Narrative*. London: Bloomsbury: T&T Clark, 1993/2015.

———. *Plotted, Shot, and Painted: Cultural Representations of Biblical Women*. Sheffield: Sheffield Academic Press, 1996.

Fern, Jessica. *Polysecure: Attachment, Trauma and Consensual Nonmonogamy*. Portland, OR: Thorntree Press, 2020.

Fischer, Irmtraud. "The Book of Ruth as Exegetical Literature." *European Judaism: A Journal for the New Europe* 40, no. 2 (2007): 140–49.

Franks, Yitzhak. *The Practical Talmud Dictionary.* Jerusalem: Ariel United Israel Institutes, 1991.

Gafney, Wil. "Mother Knows Best: Messianic Surrogacy and Sexploitation in Ruth." In *Mother Good, Mother Jones, Mommie Dearest: Biblical Mothers and Their Children*, edited by Cheryl A. Kirk-Duggan and Tina Pippin, 23–36. Atlanta: SBL, 2009.

Glueck, Norman. *Ḥesed in the Hebrew Bible*. Translated by Alfred Gottschalk. Cincinnati, OH: Hebrew Union College Press, 1967.

Graetz, Naomi. *Unlocking the Garden: A Feminist Jewish Look at the Bible, Midrash and God*. Piscataway, NJ: Gorgias Press, 2005.

Graybill, Rhiannon. *Texts After Terror: Rape Sexual Violence, and the Hebrew Bible*. Oxford: Oxford University Press, 2021.

Greenberg, Stephen. *Wresting with God and Men: Homosexuality in the Jewish Tradition*. Madison: University of Wisconsin Press, 2004.

Greenough, Chris. "'Queer Eye' in Theology and Biblical Studies: "Do You Have to be Queer to Do This?'" *Journal for Interdisciplinary Biblical Studies* 1, no. 1 (Autumn 2019): 26–41. https://jibs.hcommons.org/2022/07/20/greenough-queer-eye/#_ftn1

Greenspoon, Leonard. "Jewish Translations of the Bible." In *The Jewish Study Bible*, edited by Adele Berlin and Marc Zvi Brettler, 2005–20. Oxford: Oxford University Press, 2004.

Greenstein, Edward L. "Reading Strategies and the Story of Ruth." In *Women in the Hebrew Bible,* edited by Alice Bach, 211–31. New York: Routledge, 1999.

Guest, Deryn. "From Gender Reversal to Genderfuck: Reading Jael through a Lesbian Lens." In *Bible Trouble: Queer Reading at the Boundaries of Biblical Scholarship*, edited by Teresa J. Hornsby and Ken Stone, 9–44. Atlanta: SBL Press, 2011.

———. "Troubling the Waters: תהום, Transgender, and Reading Genesis Backwards." In *Transgender, Intersex, and Biblical Interpretation*, edited by Teresa J Hornsby and Deryn Guest. Atlanta: SBL, 2016.

———. *When Deborah Met Yael: Lesbian Biblical Hermeneutics*. London: SCM Press, 2005.

Guest, Deryn, Robert E. Goss, Mona West, and Thomas Bohache, eds. *The Queer Bible Commentary*. London: SCM Press, 2015.

Halberstam, Jack. *Female Masculinities*. Durham, NC: Duke University Press, 1998.

Harding, James E. *The Love of David and Jonathan: Ideology, Text, Reception*. Abingdon, Oxon: Taylor & Francis, 2016.

Haritaworn, Jin, Chin-ju Lin, and Christian Klesse. "Poly/logue: A Critical Introduction to Polyamory." *Sexualities* 9, no. 5 (2006): 515–29.

Haupert, M. L., Amanda N. Gesselman, Amy C. Moors, Helen E. Fisher, and Justin R. Garcia. "Prevalence of Experiences with Consensual Nonmonogamous Relationships: Findings from Two National Samples of Single Americans." *Journal of Sex and Marital Therapy* 43, no. 5 (2017): 424–40.

Hauptman, Judith. *Rereading the Rabbis: A Woman's Voice*. Boulder, CO: Westview Press, 1998.

Holtz, Barry. *Back to the Sources: Reading the Classic Jewish Texts*. New York: Simon and Schuster, 1984.

Jacobs, Louis. *The Jewish Religion: A Companion*. Oxford: Oxford University Press, 1995.

Kawashima, Robert. "Could A Woman Say 'No' in Biblical Israel? On the Genealogy of Legal Status in Biblical Law and Literature." *Association for Jewish Studies Review* 35 (2011): 1–22.

Kim, Yoo-Ki. "The Agent of Ḥesed in Naomi's Blessing (Ruth 2,20)." *Biblica* 95, no. 4 (2014): 589–60.

Knauf, Ernst A. "Shadday שדי." In *The Dictionary of Deities and Demons in the Bible*, edited by Karel van der Toorn, Bob Becking, and Pieter W. van der Horst, 1416–23. Leiden: E. J. Brill, 1995.

Koosed, Jennifer L. *Gleaning Ruth: A Biblical Heroine and Her Afterlives*. Columbia: University of South Carolina Press, 2011.

Lacocque, André. *The Feminine Unconventional: Four Subversive Figures in Israel's Tradition*. Eugene, OR: Wipf & Stock, 2005.

Lasair, Simon G. D. A. "Targum and Translation: A New Approach to a Classic Problem." *AJS Review* 34, no. 2 (2010): 265–87.

Levine, Étan. *The Aramaic Version of the Bible: Contents and Context*. Berlin: de Gruyter, 1988.

———. "Biblical Women's Marital Rights." *Proceedings of the American Academy for Jewish Research* 63 (1997): 87–135.

Lim, Timothy. "The Book of Ruth and Its Literary Voice." In *Reflection and Refraction Studies in Biblical Historiography in Honour of A. Graeme Auld*, edited by Robert Rezetko, Timothy Lim, and Brian Auker, 261–82. Leiden: Brill, 2006.

Linafelt, Tod. *Berit Olam: Ruth* and *Esther*. Collegeville, MN: Liturgical Press, 1999.

Mandolfo, Carleen R. *Daughter Zion Talks Back to the Prophets: A Dialogic Theology of the Book of Lamentations*. Atlanta: SBL, 2007.

Manion, Jen. *Female Husbands: A Trans History*. Cambridge: Cambridge University Press, 2020.

Masenya, Madipoane. "Proverbs 31:10–31 in a South African Context: A Reading for the Liberation of African (Northern Sotho) Women." In *Reading the Bible as Women: Perspectives from Africa, Asia, and Latin America* (Semeia 78), edited by Katherine Doob Sakenfeld and Sharon H. Ringe, 55–68. Atlanta: SBL, 1997.

———. "Ruth." In *Global Bible Commentary*, edited by Daniel Patte, 86–92. Nashville: Abingdon Press, 2004.

Mathias, Steffan. *Paternity, Progeny, and Perpetuation: Creating Lives After Death in the Hebrew Bible*. London: T&T Clark, 2020.

McKinley, Judith E. *Reframing Her: Biblical Women in Postcolonial Focus*. Sheffield: Sheffield Phoenix Press, 2004.

McKnight, Chris. "Polygamy and the Problem of Patriarchy." *Patheos.com*, November 7, 2017. https://www.patheos.com/blogs/hippieheretic?s=polygamy

Michaelson, Jay. "What Does the Bible Teach about Transgender People?" *The Daily Beast*, March 3, 2018. https://www.thedailybeast.com/what-does-the-bible-teach -about-transgender-people

Musa, Ayasha W. "Jael Is Non-binary; Jael Is Not a Woman." *Journal of Interdisciplinary Studies* 2, no. 1 (2020): 97–120.

Pardes, Ilana. *Countertraditions in the Bible: A Feminist Approach*. Cambridge, MA: Harvard University Press, 1992.

Paynter, Helen. *Telling Terror in Judges 19: Rape and Reparation for the Levite's Wife*. London: Routledge, 2020.

Powell, Stephanie Day. *Narrative Desire and the Book of Ruth*. London: T&T Clark, 2018.

Pyper, Hugh. "Boaz Reawakened: Modelling Masculinity in the Book of Ruth." In *Interested Readers: Essays on the Hebrew Bible in Honor of David J. A. Clines*, edited by James K. Aitken, Jeremy M. S. Clines, and Christl M. Maier, 445–58. Atlanta: SBL, 2013.

Queen-Sutherland, Kandy. *Ruth and Esther*. Macon, GA: Smyth and Helwys, 2016.

Quick, Laura. "Ruth and the Limits of Proverbial Wisdom Author(s)." *Journal of Biblical Literature* 139, no. 1 (2020): 47–66.

———. *Dress, Adornment and the Body in the Hebrew Bible*. Oxford: Oxford University Press, 2021.

Ramer, Andrew. *Queering the Text: Biblical, Medieval, and Modern Jewish Stories*. Maple Shade, NJ: Lethe Press, 2010.

Richards, Christina. "Trans and Non-Monogamies." In *Understanding Non-Monogamies*, edited by Meg Barker and Darren Langdridge, 121–33. New York: Routledge, 2009.

Ross, Samuel. "A Transgender Gaze at Genesis 38." *Journal for Interdisciplinary Biblical Studies* 2, no. 1 (Spring 2020): 25–29.

Sakenfeld, Katharine Doob. *The Meaning of Hesed in the Hebrew Bible: A New Inquiry*. Missoula, MO: Scholars Press, 1978.

Saxey, Esther. "Non-monogamy and Fiction." In *Understanding Non-Monogamies*, edited by Meg Barker and Darren Langdridge, 23–33. New York: Routledge, 2009.

Schipper, Jeremy. *The Anchor Yale Bible: Ruth—A New Translation with Introduction and Commentary*. New Haven, CT: Yale University Press, 2016.

Scholz, Susanne. *Sacred Witness: Rape in the Hebrew Bible*. Minneapolis, MN: Fortress, 2010.

Scott, James C. *Domination and the Arts of Resistance: Hidden Transcripts*. New Haven, CT: Yale University Press, 1990.

Steins, Georg. "שׁדי/sadday." In *The Theological Dictionary of the Old Testament: Volume XIV*, edited by G. Johannes Botterweck and Helmer Ringgren, 418–46. Grand Rapids, MI: William B. Eerdmans, 2004.

Steinsaltz, Rabbi Adin. *The Talmud: The Steinsaltz Edition—A Reference Guide*. New York: Random House, 1989.

Stemberger, Gunter. *Introduction to the Talmud and Midrash*. Edinburgh: T&T Clark, 1991.

Stone, Ken. *Queer Commentary and the Hebrew Bible*. London: Sheffield Phoenix Press, 2001.

Stone, Timothy. *A Compilation History of the Megilloth*. Tübingen: Mohr Siebeck, 2013.

Thiede, Barbara. *Rape Culture in the House of David*. Abingdon, Oxon: Routledge, 2022.

Trible, Phyllis. *God and the Rhetoric of Sexuality*. Philadelphia: Fortress Press, 1978.

West, Mona. "Ruth." In *The Queer Bible Commentary*, edited by Deryn Guest, Robert E. Goss, Mona West, and Thomas Bohache, 190–94. London: SCM Press, 2006.

Williamson, Robert, Jr. "Lament and the Arts of Resistance: Public and Hidden Transcripts in Lamentations 5." In *Lamentations in Ancient and Contemporary Cultural Contexts*, edited by Nancy Lee and Carleen Mandolfo, 67–80. Atlanta: SBL, 2008.

Vance, Donald R. *A Hebrew Reader for Ruth*. Peabody, MA: Hendrickson, 2003.

van Wolde, Ellen. "Intertextuality: Ruth in Dialogue with Tamar." In *A Feminist Companion to Reading the Bible: Approaches, Methods and Strategies*, edited by Athalya Brenner and Carole Fontaine, 426–51. Sheffield: Sheffield Academic Press, 1997.

———. "Sentiments as Culturally Constructed Emotions: Anger and Love in the Hebrew Bible." *Biblical Interpretation* 16 (2008): 1–24.

The Visual Commentary on Scripture: Encounter the Bible through Art. n.d. https://thevcs.org/

Wallis, Gerhard. "אָהֵב." In *The Theological Dictionary of the Old Testament Vol I* בְּדַד-אָב *(abh-badhadh)*, edited by G. Johannes Botterwick and Helmer Ringgen, 99–118. Grand Rapids, MI: William B. Eerdmans, 1977.

Weems, Renita J. *Battered Love: Marriage, Sex, and Violence in the Hebrew Prophets*. Minneapolis, MN: Fortress, 1995.

Weisberg, Dvora E. "The Widow of Our Discontent: Levirate Marriage in the Bible and Ancient Israel." *Journal for the Study of the Old Testament* 28 (2004): 403–29.

Whitley, C. F. "The Semantic Range of Ḥesed." *Biblica* 62, no. 4 (1981): 519–26.

Yamada, Frank. *Configurations of Rape in the Hebrew Bible: A Literary Analysis of Three Rape Narratives*. New York: Peter Lang, 2008.

Yee, Gale A. "'She Stood in Tears Amid the Alien Corn': Ruth, the Perpetual Foreigner and Model Minority." In *They Were All Together in One Place? Toward Minority Biblical Criticism*, edited by Randall C. Bailey, Tat-siong Benny Liew, and Fernando F. Segovia, 119–40. Atlanta: SBL, 2009.

Zobel, Hans-Jurgen. "חסד *hesed*." In *The Theological Dictionary of the Old Testament: Volume V*, edited by G. Johannes Botterweck and Helmer Ringgren, 44-64. Grand Rapids, MI: William B. Eerdmans, 1986.

Index

Note: Page numbers in italics refer to tables and figures; numbers followed by "n" refer to notes

About the Author

Rabbi Dr. Deborah Kahn-Harris is Principal of Leo Baeck College in London, where she also lectures in Hebrew Bible. Previously, she served as a rabbi at Sha'arei Tsedek North London Reform Synagogue and lectured at the School for Oriental and African Studies, University of London, where she served as the Teaching Fellow in Judaism. Her PhD thesis, "Like a Hammer for Shattering Rock: Employing Classical Rabbinic Hermeneutics to Fashion Contemporary Feminist Commentary on the Bible," was completed at the University of Sheffield.

9 781666 932096